WATCHING THE DETECTIVES

WATCHING THE DETECTIVES

Andrew Brown

Hodder & Stoughton
LONDON SYDNEY AUCKLAND TORONTO

British Library Cataloguing in Publication Data

Brown, Andrew
    Watching the Detectives.
    1. Metropolitan Police
    I. Title
    363.2′ 092′ 4   HV8196.L6

    ISBN 0-340-39695-4

CONTENTS

ACKNOWLEDGEMENTS

The verses on pp 71-2 are quoted by permission of A.P. Watt Ltd on behalf of the executors of the estate of Robert Graves.

The lines on p 88 are reprinted by permission of Faber & Faber Ltd from *The Collected Poems 1909-1962* by T.S. Eliot.

WATCHING THE DETECTIVES

Foreword

This book started, I suppose, with a traffic accident in May 1985. I think someone was killed then, but I didn't get close enough to see, since a crowd of passers-by had coagulated around the shiny metal at the junction of Queensway and the Bayswater Road, and three of the policemen who had arrived at the scene were cajoling and pushing away the spectators. The fourth was able to try and do something useful for the victims before the ambulance arrived. And I wondered how it must feel to serve a public like that.

Later that summer I did a story for the *Spectator* about the police in Newham, where a systematic method for dealing with racial harassment had been worked out by an inspector. I had avoided police stations on principle ever since spending some time I'd rather not have done in one in the West of Ireland when I was about seventeen and fond of drugs. My parents got me out of that mess, which is one of the smaller debts I owe them.

At first, the station in Newham seemed just as one would expect, if anyone from West London can expect what he finds east of the River Lea. I arrived late, having misunderstood my instructions, and was put to wait in an interrogation room smelling of disinfectant and cigarette ash. Eventually, I reached the place I should have been, and met an officer who talked like a man from the Treasury, as if he feared that his solutions might fail because they were too elegant for the world outside. The tea in his office was served in exquisite cups. I had neither expected this, nor been capable of imagining it.

I passed rapidly down the line to the inspector who

devised the system, and who seemed surprised that anyone from the press should seem interested in what was fundamentally no more than a new sort of internal police paperwork. Then the press officer and I went out with one of the Home Beat officers on whose reports the whole system depended.

I can't now remember much of what happened on an uneventful walk through a council estate which seemed to have grown steadily more squalid and shabby since it was built about twenty-five years ago, except for the children's voices singing 'Old Bill' in a derisive chorus, from somewhere above our heads, as we checked out a flat from which a family of mixed race had been driven out by having turds pushed through their letterbox and similar gestures of neighbourly concern. That story appeared, and was fairly good; but inadequate. I had caught what happened, but not how these people had talked, nor how they had seemed to think.

I wanted to find out how London looked from underneath a helmet. This happily found phrase allowed plans for a book to grow clearer. I would have to find a part of London I had not seen before, so that my eyes were fresh; and if the things I saw were to be representative, it would have to be a mixed part of the city, ranging from the suburbs to the slums. On the other hand, it could not be too big if there were to be any chance of striking up a personal rapport with a significant number of policemen there within the four months allotted for research. I think I was also afraid that too small an area might not have enough interesting crimes.

As I talked this over with my agent, Xandra Hardie, in the autumn of 1985, the Met was just phasing out its old organisational structure in which London was divided into lettered districts. J District, which was the one we decided I should study, consisted of ten stations which covered roughly the area served by the eastern extension of the

Central Line, from Loughton on the edge of Epping Forest to Walthamstow on the edge of the 'inner city' belt.

On the tube map of London, this is one of the tentacular extensions outside the yellow ring of the Circle Line which no one knows unless they have to live there. It belongs to a different world from west London: one not necessarily less prosperous, and in many ways rather nicer. But one of the unspoken and perhaps unspeakable conventions which give cities their character stipulates that no one with my accent would think of living out there. One of the minor pleasures of writing this book was learning to appreciate such a foreign part of London. Whether it has any great internal cohesion I do not know: politically, it ranges from the hard-left council in Hackney to Norman Tebbit's constituency of Chingford, where you will see Mercedes parked outside the porticoes built on to council houses bought by their tenants. I think J Division is the single most varied patch of London in the Met, though the old K Division, which forms a wedge south of J from Romford into Newham, must be nearly as diverse.

Part of the synopsis I wrote for Hodder & Stoughton shows what I thought I would accomplish:

> The murder of PC Blakelock - and Bernie Grant's reaction to this atrocious crime – mark a significant moment in modern British history. What makes this episode uniquely shocking and important is that it shows the extent to which arguments about policing are in the last resort arguments about the proper morality of society.
>
> Stories of the police vary dramatically according to the teller's fears, sufferings, or prejudices. That is not good enough. It is vital to find out by a detailed and intimate study what ordinary policemen think and feel about their job, and why they do so; and to

13

present it in a way which will attract and enlighten the reader.

The book will be written in the form of a traditional precinct-based police fiction – like an Ed McBain novel or *Hill Street Blues*. But it will deal with the actual experiences of individual policemen in a particular division of the Met.

J Division will give a very wide range of policing problems, which is essential to the scheme of the book. The police come to their more glamorous jobs conditioned by their experience of unspeakably dreary work, like chasing unsolvable burglaries. This range provides in turn the structure of the book; one chapter to each type of crime. This structure allows the development of different police characters, since no single policeman can be intimately involved with all the different sorts of work required by an area as large as the one I will deal with.

The crimes I will write about are those which are interesting either because they are spectacular, or because they mean so much to their victims: racial harassment, burglary, violence, possibly murder, drugs and sex offences. There are also the topics which are important to the police themselves: the issue and use of firearms, the stress on family life, promotion and pay. These will be dealt with, like the crimes, by illustrating and arranging them around particular cases.

The way I now propose to work is three weeks on and one week off (doing some quite different story) for the duration of the research period. Not all of the 'on' time would be spent in police company: there is a certain amount of historical and legal research which must be done, and I would also hope to get to know how different some of the areas feel when they are seen alone.

This method has the further advantage of giving a time perspective. The length of time before you see the results of your work is something that differs greatly from job to job, and gives these jobs much of their character. It is an important part of my idea that one should be able to follow the progress of long investigations, rather than the sort of smash bang wallop action served up on television.

Three months of prodding the press office for permission produced no result, until suddenly I received an invitation to see the Deputy Assistant Commissioner in charge of the area. I stuttered for about ten minutes when asked what I was trying to do. Then he said it would be fine, and made the necessary arrangements. I signed various forms absolving the Force from responsibility for anything that might happen to me while in their vehicles, and spent four months working my way around most of the stations of J District, starting in Ilford.

One

Adventures in the Pink Neon Zone

'We have a saying in the East End' – the chief superintendent looked at me with large brown eyes behind thick
spectacles, anxious to be correctly understood – 'that if
you let a dog through your front door, he'll shit on the
carpet. And to be honest, Andrew, if it were up to me, I
wouldn't have you here. But I have been told to do it, and
I will. Besides, I'm interested in people. Now, you
wouldn't quote that, would you?'

I said of course I would, because I'm interested in
language; but that he'd be anonymous.

'What would you do if you were out with the lads, and
you saw one of them punch a prisoner right in the face?
You might misunderstand a thing like that. I mean,
perhaps the prisoner had himself swung a punch around
the corner where you couldn't see it . . .'

I dithered for a while. It was not a question I'd expected
in that form. Eventually, I told him I'd complain to him
first, and then see what would happen. He smiled with
real pleasure: 'There, you see. That was a bit of a trick
question. Because I've been here two years now, and I've
never had a single complaint of that sort of thing.'

On the outside of his door was a small, yellowed
rectangle of newsprint, curling from under the Sellotape:
'Never demand as a right what you can ask as a favour'.
On the inside, was a poster of a chimpanzee complaining
that 'Every time I find the solution, they change the
problem'. His trophy cabinet – something that all senior

16

officers seem to acquire – was surmounted by two carved wooden hands, one with a finger raised at the world, one with two. In such surroundings it seemed foolish to look for the uniform one expects policemen to wear beneath the skin. Not until I met 'the puggy man' later and stood like a policeman in his blood-stained living room did I realise that a uniform can mean only what other people want it to.

One of the press officers involved in the preliminary negotiations had been very keen that I should start by doing night shifts in an Area Car: one of the big Rovers which zoom around answering 999 calls. He was anxious that I should see the glamorous side of police work. In the event, I found instead how chaotic things can be. This was a more useful lesson.

On my first night I arrived at Ilford at around 5.30, to find normal confusion. A new black cop was on duty at the desk, a young one named Norman Clarke. He kept me waiting at the counter, having forgotten that there was meant to be an author around. He was very polite about this but, as a probationer, anxious to do the right thing and unsure what this might be when it involved dealing with the public. His manner in the canteen, where I awaited the crew of Juliet 3, was anxious and ingratiating; but it was to be very self-assured on the job, as will emerge.

Juliet 3 was a large Rover, white, with a blue lamp on top, but without the adornments of traffic cars or pandas: it had no stop sign, and the police flashes were reasonably discreet. These cars are unpopular with most of their drivers: the best people will say of them is that they look the part, and that they are fast once they get going. But their size makes them unwieldy in city streets, and their acceleration is not tremendous.

The driver was John Miller, a moustachioed Geordie

with eleven years' service; the navigator, Paul Murphy, known as 'Murph', an undernourished haystack.

By 6.30, after a meal in the canteen, we were ready to go. As we pulled out of the station a message came through – an 'IC1' (white male), wearing a black jacket and carrying a white bag, had been seen leaping over a wall to escape from a church.

Immediately, we start moving faster than I would have thought possible. Except at roundabouts, the siren noise was left behind us, and even these were taken at thirty miles an hour in short four-wheel drifts. At one stage we hit 90 m.p.h in a thirty-mile limit.

Arriving at the church, we scrambled clumsily but quickly over a stone wall, ignoring the locked gate, and started moving through the yard. There was no point in running, since we didn't know what we were after, but this quiet motion, listening to the scuff of boots on asphalt, was much more exciting than the noisy whirlwind drive, since we did not know who was in there, nor what would happen if we found them.

There was no one. Nothing happened; the church windows were unbroken, and though we found the man who had rung in the call, who confirmed all the essential details, all he saw was a bloke vaulting over a wall. There was a perfectly ordinary and very much simpler alleyway available, but there was no evidence of any crime having been committed.

So that they can respond to 999 calls the main radios of the Area Cars are tuned to Scotland Yard, where a 'despatcher' is handed incoherent messages from the public and converts them to a standardised form, read out in tones of infinite weariness. Frequently, these are directed to particular cars. The driver also carries a personal radio, which is tuned into the station frequency, and carries less urgent messages.

As we cruised round, looking for stolen cars or 'pollack'

– young ladies going about their lawful business in a decorative manner – we had a call to return to the station, to deliver Norman Clarke to the mortuary. This is not what Area Cars ought really to do, but it would take little time, and perhaps the car crew were trying, slightly, to wind me up. A woman had died in West Ham, but had been taken to the mortuary here, so both police stations were involved in dealing with the death.

She had been old – about seventy-five perhaps. Her skin was not waxy but had the dull, off-right colour of cheap plastic flowers; the eyelids had crumpled to expose lustreless eyeballs. One sensible white woollen sock had been rolled down from her knee over a sensible black shoe; 'DELAFORCE' had been written up one short white calf in black felt-pen – sensibly enough, Norman took notes. The rest of us were silent in the cold, sweetish mortuary smell.

We left him there, and in the car lit cigarettes. Policing is 90 per cent common sense. Around us the Victorian tombstones stretched like dirty white teeth into the darkness beyond the headlights. 'Thomas Surety', one said, like a promise.

'That's one of the worst parts of the job.' John Miller said, 'specially when they've been dead for a few weeks, and the maggots have got at them . . . Then we have to send the fishermen, and they take the tobacco tins . . .'

I laughed and said foolishly that nurses cultivated the same sense of humour, for the same reasons. Foolishly, because nurses are women, and because only policemen have the most important job in the world.

By now it was fully dark. John drove us slowly round the monied streets of Wanstead, looking for burglars.

'Look at that drum: it's like something out of the bloody Addams family.'

Seeing nothing, we pulled off on to a dirt track across the park to bump along, trying to catch sex maniacs, or, failing that, to trap rabbits in the headlights. The conversation wandered to Broadwater Farm. Like any policeman who had read WPS Meynell's report, John felt that the working police had been betrayed by their superior officers. He'd learnt of PC Blakelock's death from a journalist, after the police radio had explicitly denied that there had been any serious injuries. 'It's a pity they didn't finish what they were doing, and cut his head right off, and parade it round on a pole. I know it sounds dreadful. But that's what they were going to do; and if they'd done it, then everyone would know what they were like. But they only got half-way through the neck . . . people still don't realise what we're up against.'

Then at half-past eight we were called to a drugs case in a pub, over the local radio. We parked around the corner, by a panda car, from which two young men in civilian clothes emerged, I looked for their escorts, but one of them came over to the car, and I realised they were themselves police. He leant in and spoke urgently: the landlord had phoned to say that 'two Herberts' were 'standing by the cigarette machine and joshing out drugs of some description'.

The plain-clothes men hurried away to investigate; one returned after a quarter of an hour. While we waited, the radio asked if we knew what it was all about. John said yes, but it was nice of them to ask. He grumbled quietly about the job. 'Morale is lower now than it's ever been since I joined the force . . . it's not the same job as the one I joined, and it's not so good. Since they brought in PACE [the Police and Criminal Evidence Act – in his Geordie accent, the word sounded like 'piss'] we're moving towards something like the Miranda system in the States, which is dreadful . . . the Commissioner in his infinite wisdom has decided that everything should be decent. Then they shift you around every five years. It's really difficult for someone like Murph to specialise . . .

But the unpredictability of this job is the best thing. You can do what you like within limits.'

Murph walked to the off-licence and bought a tube of peppermints while we waited, and shared them around. He spoke little in Miller's presence – after all, he had nine years' less service – but now he, too, felt emboldened to grumble:

'You're a policeman on the streets. You're not a policeman in an office. ' It was clearly a ritual incantation.

'For a bloke with my service,' said John, 'I'm still fairly keen; and I like to think that I'm fairly good.' Just then, the plain-clothes man walked silently to his door, and rapped on the window.

He'd started to speak before he saw me, and had to be quickly reassured about my presence. 'They're talking about sulphate a lot,' he said, 'But I can't see them dealing anything. The landlord says they were passing white packets around half an hour ago. I don't know whether to do them now, or to wait for evidence of supply. It would be better for everybody if we could do that. But I want to do them before the pub gets too crowded.'

He returned: I waited five more minutes, then followed him.

From Edmonton to Dagenham, smart pubs are all the same. Pink neon signs in curling script, with green neon decorative flourishes crowning their extensions, which are made from concrete slabs. They all sell food – chile con carne, variously spelt, but made from the same gritty mince and served on slabs of tepid rice – and cocktails with plastic decorations standing in thick pastel liqueurs. The drinkers enjoy themselves hugely; they have come to be smart and successful, and later to fight.

Within the bar, the two cops stood by a mirrored pillar, looking like any East End youths on a Friday night. One wore a grey-brown bomber jacket with a tweed lining, open to reveal a pastel-striped shirt over bleached jeans and white trainers; the other had pressed grey slacks and a chrome-yellow pullover.

The suspects lounged and laughed in chairs, having a fairly quiet, and to all appearances enjoyable, night out. Two would call themselves black, being the colour of coffee made with condensed milk; the other three were white. All were male, and none looked particularly druggy.

At 9.04 the dark-haired policeman slipped out to brief the reinforcements he had summoned. Within four minutes he returned and trotted up the stairs to the dais on which the young men sat. He leant over their table like a solicitous waiter, holding his warrant card. By the time I could hear him speaking, four uniformed policemen were trotting up the stairs in line. There was a very brief altercation, and everyone filed out again. The first suspect was outside the pub before anyone realised what had happened. Just as I left the bar after the last policeman the sound of conversation changed, like the noise of a brook when a stone is pulled from its bed.

Outside, the suspects had been lined up against the wall of the pub. Voices sounded loud and hard beneath the concrete overhang. The tall, pale black – taller than any policeman – was found to have a small chunk of hash in a pocket. The others were all clean. The short black became aggressive, and considered himself harassed. An older policeman with a mottled red nose like a traffic cone, one of the reinforcements, told him to shut up or he would be arrested too.

'What for? I ain't done nothing.'

'Drunk and disorderly.'

'Come on, man, you can't do that. I've only had a couple of drinks.'

'Yes I can. Come on over here.'

He pulled away from the action, and they argued out of

earshot by one of the cars. There was some further hassle between John and the arrested black about an anorak: John reluctant to let go of his arm to allow him to put it on. Eventually they moved in an uncomfortable shuffle to the panda car, telling the friend, by now released, that they were taking him to Ilford.

'Think you're doing a good job, do you?' said the friend to me, with something between a sneer and a tease. I did not.

Yet back at the station, all was cool and almost jokey with the release of tension. The piece of dope, in a little polythene bag, was smaller than my fingernail, though about an eighth of an inch thick.

'How much d'you pay for that?' asked the charging sergeant.

'A fiver.'

She looked genuinely shocked.

'Yeah, but I smoked some.' He smiled. By now there was some sense of people joshing each other.

'Who was in there? You and him?'

'Yeah. We didn't see you all.'

'We were really close to you. We heard you talking about sulphate and all that.' The prisoner smiled reminiscently.

'We thought you had about two kilos of heroin on you.' When the fair-haired plain-clothes man smiled he looked suddenly like Tintin.

'How d'you spell hashish?' asked the dark one as we entered the interview room, which was uncomfortably hot, and painted an even pastel green that still seemed lavatorial. High on the wall behind him was a window of small panes of frosted glass which looked like those skylights which separate a basement from the street. Two tables had been pushed together against one wall with an office typewriter in the middle. The dark plain-clothes man had a heap of interview forms in front of him; the

23

prisoner sat opposite, beyond the typewriter; the fair policeman lounged, facing the terrible machine.

I had read typed interview transcripts before. At times they seemed to have come from an unpublished draft of *The Waste Land*: the answers were demotic, rendered accurately and without punctuation, in short lines corresponding to the handwritten originals; the questions plodding and careful. What the transcripts omitted were the pauses after each answer when the only sound was the quick rustle of the interviewer's hand moving across the paper between the words that he was writing down with a cheap biro. In fact it was this writing that supplied the only sinister note in the interview. It is done to safeguard the prisoner's rights: when all is over he must sign every single reply and every alteration to confirm that it is what he said. But, as any journalist knows, the act of writing down anyone's speech makes them very uneasy. It may be ludicrous to worry about words when in trouble for deeds, but people do. There was far more apprehension on the prisoner's face as the last long question was being written down as it was asked than when he was being arrested.

On the other hand, any journalist would envy a policeman's painstaking freedom to get it right, without worrying about boring his victim:

Can you tell me where you bought that from?
Yeah, Sandringham Road.
Is that in Hackney?
Yeah.
Whereabouts in Sandringham Road did you buy it?
A caff, Ossies.
Who did you buy it from?
Yellowman.
What was that?
Yellowman they call him.
Who calls him that?

Everybody.

Why?

'Cause he's yellow.

What is he? Chinese, or Japanese, or what?

No, he's half-caste. But he's really very light-skinned.

Do you know his real name?

No.

How long ago did you buy it?

Tuesday.

Do you remember what time of day?

Evening, night time.

. . . .

Does Yellowman sell any other types of drugs that you know about?

Just hash and cannabis weed.

D'you drink in the Xxxx pub often?

No. This was the first time.

What made you decide to go there tonight?

'Cause we were meeting to go up to Camden Palace.

How well do you know the boys you were drinking with tonight?

I went to school with two of them.

Which ones? You don't . . . We've got their names anyway.

Bert and Simon.

Which school?

[illegible]

Did any of them have any drugs tonight?

No.

Are you sure about that?

Yeah.

Was the piece of hash that you had tonight for your own use?

Yeah.

25

So: had any of you been dealing drugs in the pub before we got there?

No.

Do you know anyone in that pub who sells drugs?

No.

The interviewer looked up and asked his colleague: 'Can you think of any more questions?' The fair-haired policeman, who had been sitting with a finger under his ear, stroking his chin, said no, he thought that covered everything. There was a silence that seemed very long while the final question was written out. When all was signed, the dark-haired policeman grinned, and said at a normal pace:

'Magic! Well done, mate.'

It's curious, but when the police address you by your Christian name, this is a sign that they mistrust you. One of the first things done during any arrest is to ask the suspect what he wants to be called, or what his mates call him. This gets a little contact going immediately. But once the police relax, they go back to more general terms, like 'mate'.

While the last arrangements were being made for Michael to return in six weeks' time to hear the result of the analysis and to learn if he would be charged, I brooded on the prejudices involved. Arresting blacks for the possession of trivial amounts of dope is meant to be one of the classic forms of police harassment. But who had shown prejudice in this episode?

The policemen had been told these people were dealing in drugs. Their informant was the landlord, and, coming from such a source, the information could not have been discounted. They had heard enough to decide – quite rightly – that the suspects all used illegal drugs, even if they weren't 'joshing them out' in public. So they had a

26

duty to do something. They were also expecting trouble, and afraid of it.

Perhaps it was prejudiced of them to expect trouble – in other words, violent resistance – at the arrest; but the expectation of trouble is founded on a judgement about the suspect's respect for the authority of the police. After Broadwater Farm, there is no predisposition to suppose that black, drug-dealing youths are burdened with such respect.

But these suspects were not in fact dealing. They hardly had anything on them; and once this became apparent the whole situation calmed down. The black who was not arrested expected the police to be hostile: that was a form of prejudice, though the policeman who threatened him with arrest for drunk and disorderly was both hostile and expecting hostility. But he did not make the arrest; everyone managed to stick to the rules. This was just as well for me, since I could never have testified that the short black man was anything like drunk.

Everyone in fact behaved according to their expectations, which were all, to start off with, false: the police thought they were arresting dealers; the suspects that they were having a quiet night out. These expectations were founded on a specific item of information: the landlord's report that the two blacks had been handing out white packets by the cigarette machine (Michael had only £10 on him, so if it were true, it would be interesting to know where the profits had gone). It is perhaps germane that the two black suspects were the only blacks among perhaps 100 customers in the pub, and that this was their first visit there. If I were looking for prejudice in this story, that is where would I look.

There was a commotion in the anteroom outside the charge-room: a short passage with benches on each side, and no handle on the outer door. One could not see clearly through the small panes of thickly rippled glass

27

which separated the two rooms; a great deal of swearing could be heard coming from the tenebrous shapes beyond. The door opened inwards and a large policeman marched through, gripping by the elbow a handcuffed youth. The new prisoner had luxuriant fox-red hair and hot blue eyes, and the dead-white complexion of extreme drunken anger. There was blood on his elbows and down the thighs of his pale denim trousers; one of the six escorting policemen had blood all down one arm, which he waved at a WPC who was fingering a nail she had broken in the fight. The bright steel handcuffs were all that seemed clean in the room. All of the newcomers were panting; the foxy youth could hardly stand for drink, but still burnt with an incandescent lust to savage. I watched him weighing his chances, in handcuffs, against six policemen. They watched him too, and when he'd quietened down, brought in his two companions.

All were sat down on a bench and told to shut up: they began to quarrel among themselves, in low, angry voices, while the charging sergeant typed out the necessary forms, using one finger. They had been fighting in one of the local pubs, and when the police arrived had fallen on these new enemies with delight.

In the ten minutes it took to fill out the forms, the companions had lost their pallor and begun to sober up slightly. The foxy youth had not. He was made to stand in front of the desk and his handcuffs were removed.

'That fucking hurts, copper.'

'It does, doesn't it,' said one of the bloody policemen, unmoved. The rufous man lurched around the front of the room, and refused to give his name. All his aggression now seemed directed against his companions, and theirs against him:

'Shut up, cunt.'

'Who're you calling cunt, you fucking bastard. Shut the fuck up.'

28

'Fucking shut up yourself,'

'You stupid cunt. Wait till we get out of here. I'll fucking get you.'

'Fucking shut up, you drunken wanker.' The boy on the bench who shouted that would not have done so without the police in the room to protect him from his friend, who then became obsessed by the idea that people thought he might not be sober.

'I'm not fucking drunk!' he kept shouting, 'Fucking bastard coppers. You can't do me for drunk and disorderly. I'm not fucking drunk.'

'You are, cunt,' from the bench.

Still shouting, he was led off to the cells. There was no point in even trying to charge him. From the other youths, by now quite subdued and embarrassed, it emerged that they were all seventeen. None of them could remember why they had been fighting, or whom.

The foxy youth could still be heard yelling from the cells that he wasn't fucking drunk; and now the other prisoners were yelling too; several demanding that he shut up; most of the rest demanding that the police beat him into silence; one prisoner, more imaginative than the rest, asking to be put in a cell with him.

The charging sergeant looked at me: 'I almost wish we could,' she said.

It was now 10.30: the crew of Juliet 3 were due to change. I met their replacements at 11.05: Peter Conn, a saturnine PC with twenty years' service and Rachel, a WPC in her late twenties (even policemen think policemen are young nowadays) with dark hair and an outdoor complexion.

Peter was a less flamboyant driver than John Miller, but very quick indeed. At 11.44, as we were cruising up the North Circular Road in search of a yellow Triumph Stag and a red Lotus, which had been reported by an off-duty PC as containing a gang armed with baseball bats, a call came through from Dagenham: 'Urgent assistance.'

He pulled up calmly at the next roundabout, switched on the blue light, and turned right directly into the other carriageway. We started hurtling through the night once more, this time without skids or drama, and sometimes with the siren switched off. The handwriting in my notebook jagged and leapt to form a word I later deciphered as 'restful'.

Eight miles and ten minutes later we approached the last roundabout, wailing and flashing. A battered Ford Escort pulled up to let us through – and nearly got crumpled by a white Transit full of still more policemen who had had a four-mile start on us; then the radio told us to relax, and it was all over. A PC had tried to stop two drunks in a car, and been dragged along beside it, as we learnt as we were drinking tea in the car at the back of Chadwell Heath police station.

At 12.17, four sips into the tea, the radio went off again: robbery in progress at a petrol station four miles away.

'All right,' said Rachel, enthusiastically, and reached for the light switch, Peter jumped out, dumped the cups, and this time we drove even faster. But Juliet 4, the other Area Car, just beat us to the scene: three men armed with iron bars had threatened the cashier, and made off in a blue Cortina. They were caught the next day in Leyton-stone, with their balaclavas and their iron bars still in the boot, by an off-duty officer who recognised the car and followed it in his own. But there was nothing for us to do that evening except cruise around the back streets trying to guess which way they had escaped, until, after only three minutes of this, an even better call came through: 'Suspects on premises' in a shopping centre.

We overshot the building society; the only pedestrian on the street ran up, pointing us ten yards backwards, and there we saw a broken glass panel at the bottom of an office door. We ducked underneath and started to run through the deserted building, switching on lights, testing doors, and hearing more and more policemen arrive. I had thought I was frightened of what would happen if we found the suspects; but, pounding up and down the stairs behind Rachel, I realised I was more worried they would disappear.

It seemed for a while that they had done so. Then the dog found them out on the roof, and off we ran again. I followed Rachel round the block to cut off the escape from the back; we scrambled on to a ten-foot wall, and saw at the other end a human silhouette: 'They're not here!' he called. 'Oh shit,' said Rachel, 'I've ripped my trousers.'

More walking round, not panting now, but swinging torches into alleyways: the burglars could apparently be heard, but not seen, on a pent roof adjoining the flat roof, on to where they had originally escaped. Then a dark bulk and a white shape moved against a chimney 100 feet above ground, and we realised that they could not come down.

By this time there was quite a crowd on the shopping street, in the cold wind: fifteen or twenty policemen, clumps of as many youths on their way home from the pub; and the inspector had summoned a fire engine.

The roof was steep and slippery, stretching down for about twenty feet on each side of the coping, and though the burglars had worked their way past five chimney stacks, no policeman was going to follow them.

The first fire engine had only an aluminium ladder which swayed and bounced as the inspector climbed up it. But when he reached the edge of the roof, the burglars would not come down. By now there were lights shining on them all the time: they wore thin bum-freezer jackets, like any young men in Ilford, and they must have been extremely

31

cold. The street beneath them was full of fire engines and policemen; an impulsive burglary which would hardly have netted them anything had turned into the best news of the week. They would not come down.

The second fire engine had a hydraulic platform, with a searchlight mounted underneath it. Peter Conn climbed in with another policeman, and after some minutes of futile arguing was swung to the next chimney stack along, where they scrambled out, and then edged their way round. The dark shapes beyond were just humps in the shadow; the red glow from Peter's cigarette waxed and dimmed, then scuttled and bumped towards the final chimney stack. He leant round, and offered the two burglars a cigarette. Now there were three red glowings on the roof, and an indistinguishable conversation; five minutes later, they'd all been lowered to the ground in the platform. It had taken an hour since they were first found on the roof.

I was wondering how this story could possibly be told – how the danger could be disentangled from the glamour – when Rachel appeared at my side and asked if I wanted a murder: which is how I first met Inspector Thompson.

'Authoring doesn't seem to keep you fit,' he said with some relish as I pounded up to his car. We drove smoothly to a quiet street of semi-detached houses in Wanstead, then walked in quick confusion for five minutes, trying to find the right house. A girl had stabbed her boyfriend there an hour before. No one knew if he would live, and he was not expected to. Inspector Thompson's job was to preserve the evidence; the sergeant who drove us explained that there was blood all over the hall floor and living-room carpet. When we arrived, there was nothing but a wet floor-cloth on the hall linoleum. The man who let us in held a scrubbing brush in his hand. He was balding and stocky, with large hands and a pale, creased, puggy face.

'I'm just cleaning where they spilt the beer,' he asserted, showing us a great discoloration on the living-room carpet, by a galvanised bucket. Some threads of blood remained on a cream armchair.

'I wouldn't mess up any evidence. Look: there's the beer they were drinking.' He pointed to a yellow plastic crate with the empties neatly stacked among full bottles.

'Did you put those back?'

'Yes, I was just tidying up.'

'There might have been fingerprints on them.' Thompson's most usual voice is a drawl which gives the impression that he is rather amused by everything, and very much in control of it. When this control seems threatened, his voice rises a little in pitch, and becomes clipped and clear: 'A pointless sacrifice is just what the war needs at this stage, Carruthers.' But for the moment he just sounded tired: the puggy man needed no encouragement to make a pointless effort. The difficulty was to remember that anything might have a point at half-past two on a Saturday morning, with nearly four hours of the shift still to run.

The puggy man started to give his version of what had happened: his daughter was violently against drugs, as she had to be, since her twin brother was a junkie; and this coloured boy had brought some into the house. Now he had nothing against coloured kids, he was not a racist or anything, but everyone knows they use a lot of drugs, and his daughter wouldn't have anything to do with them. No; she hated drugs – but this boy had started smoking them in the house. He himself didn't know anything about it. He'd not been in the room. But the way he'd heard it, she had objected to this, and her boyfriend had got violent. When he came down the stairs they were fighting. Here was the beer bottle he had taken from the coloured boy. And then she'd stabbed him: yes she had, but doubtless she'd had her reasons.

While he delivered this speech his earnest eyes set in a pale face jumped round our faces like an anxious dog. His hands kept moving, tidying away the débris of the crime, as if when all the blood was gone the stabbing, too, would have been mopped away. The sergeant stood very still, which in that cluttered room seemed an aggressive gesture; Thompson's manner suggested infinite comprehension and fatigue:

'Well, you'd best leave the room as it is. The fingerprint people will be round in the morning. In the meantime you'd better try to get some sleep.'

'It's so hard to get to sleep after things like this. That's the trouble — '

The puggy man spoke with real surprise.

Back at the station I asked Thompson what drugs he thought the boys on the roof had taken. By now he was quite yellow with fatigue; his face seemed assembled from crumpled cigar leaves, as he sprawled along a home office issue chair in the reserve room:

'They've just got no respect for the law, and no respect for any sort of authority.'

It seemed an inadequate answer – but we were interrupted by a voice at the counter in the room behind us. A lean and prosperous looking man stood there, complaining that his gold Ford Granada had been stolen. He wore two gold medallions round his neck. I felt that I was expected to be astonished, so I walked round to the side door and peered through the small window there. This time, I could see that he was wearing white satin underpants with blue piping, and a gold football manager's bracelet. Nothing else. The PC at the desk seemed quite impassive while the prosperous man explained that the car was now being chased through the streets of Ilford by a hamburger van.

In a world where such things happen, and no one involved thinks them the least ridiculous, what better guide for conduct than authority?

TWO

Watching The Public

Sir Kenneth Newman believes that the essential quality of police work is the use of force: a policeman may for most of his working life be functionally indistinguishable from a social worker or a second-rate typist, yet in the last analysis he is authorised to compel others to behave as they would rather not, and indeed must compel them. All other civil order depends on this.

Yet police on the ground are much more concerned with the exercise of authority than with force. I do not mean by this to imply that Sir Kenneth Newman is an unnaturally violent man; just that his position requires the sort of fundamental thinking which ordinary policemen can be glad to evade. The craft of old-fashioned policing was based around the use of authority as a substitute for force: the middle-aged, ponderous constable who never, ever, ran to break up fights did not merely preserve himself from harm; he built up the idea that policemen could not be hurt, which tended to protect them. But nowadays the young PCs in Leyton are taught never to turn their backs on trouble lest a knife be used; the old accepted rules are gone, and with them the old style of policing. Sir Kenneth Newman himself is engaged in an attempt to transform the way in which the Met thinks of itself: policing is to be less a function of society than the management of an organisation. This change involves, among other things, the adoption of a more open style of command in which less can be taken for granted, more must be explained; but this has had to be imposed on a fairly reluctant Force. The problem involved is not that senior officers are reluctant to take the men into their confidence: it's that the older sort of PC would rather not think about the horrors of his job.

It may seem that the riots of recent years have made force a more prominent part of policing; but they have also exposed the inadequacy of physical violence as a means of police control. It is only soldiers who are expected to attain their ends by force alone, and even they, if well led, will care as much for their moral ascendancy as for their physical prowess. A battle in which the enemy surrenders is a greater victory than one in which he must be killed. Even those policemen who enjoy the use of force recognise its limits: an inspector who had learnt his trade in Holloway (which is rougher than much of the East End) and who had nothing against an honest fist fight as one means of establishing a moral ascendancy over a turbulent pub said to me one evening (in a quiet pub) that twenty men, properly led, were all you would ever need to quell a disturbance. If twenty unarmed policemen couldn't handle the trouble, 200 would be just as insufficient.

Football matches show these problems of force and authority very clearly. The game remains a genuine popular ritual to an extent which those who do not go to matches cannot expect to understand. If attendance at a game is considered as a ritual, it has its own rules which are both accepted and partially invented by the participants: no need of force here. But any crowd has a capacity for violence, the more frightening because it is largely unconscious: to see the work which spontaneous merriment entails for the police, walk through Trafalgar Square in the afternoon of New Year's Eve and count the crush barriers. And sporting crowds are much more openly aggressive. Even to watch a football match on a pub television set is to hear shouts of 'kick his legs off'. At a real ground middle-aged ladies shriek as if at wrestling matches, while the fine spittle flying from their lips coats like dandruff the uniformed shoulders of the policemen beneath.

The hooligans themselves are a smaller and more specialised problem. They are just 'yobs' in police terminology, though these yobs are defiling something valuable, since football offers for many policemen a respectable pleasure (Mr Robinson has a season ticket to the Arsenal; Inspector Thompson follows Tottenham). When the two teams played each other on Good Friday, only Inspector Thompson was present, and he was working. He had been since a quarter to seven that morning, when he paraded a 'serial' (twenty PCs and two sergeants) at Wanstead.

Wanstead is a small, Victorian station that overlooks a village green. The garden once won a prize; the main office has the cold smell of old stations, compounded of dust and sweaty uniforms and cigarette ash. In the middle of the night, when the Area Car comes in for tea, you feel you are calling on an outpost of the Foreign Legion. The area around is so quiet and respectable that it seems in policing terms a desert. Thick-throated from cigarettes instead of sleep, I counted, the first time I came there, the evidence of others' cafard: the exhortatory notice from Sir Kenneth Newman which had been altered from 'Force goals' to read 'own goals'; a poster advertising vasectomies, to which had been appended a scornful macho commentary; the desk man ordering a crime book, arguing lethargically with his partner about how the paperwork should be done.

The morning of the match, though, was full of bustling inactivity. The small station room was crammed: the doors blocked with policemen's backs, and the policemen chosen all seemed unusually tall. It was the best time of

37

the morning, for within half an hour we were all crammed into two vans: a hired minibus, and a Ford Transit 'carrier'.

The carriers are bare, functional, and unpleasant. At that time, they usually held the District Support Units, mobile squads kept in reserve for special tasks. To ride in these, with their long periods of boredom and discomfort interrupted only by sudden anti-climaxes, is to understand how surprising it is that more policemen do not go sour. There is a special quality of frustration in these carriers, which arises from the fact that policemen like their jobs. They will tolerate inaction if that is what the situation calls for: most of their work at a football match is simply to stand around and be conspicuous. That may not be exciting, but it is good police work. In a carrier, on the other hand, you spend much time doing nothing, yet knowing there are things you should be doing. London is full of emergencies: the radio is tuned to Scotland Yard's 999 call broadcasts, and these represent only a fraction of the potential 999 calls; yet any given carrier is almost certain to be doing nothing at any given time.

I had perhaps the best seat, with no one in front of me and room for my legs behind the riot shields strapped to the floor at the front of the passenger compartment. Everyone else was crammed on bench seats. Inspector Thompson, a sergeant and the driver all squeezed into the front. The conversation in the back was coarse for a while, with Karen Gilmour from the burglary squad fielding ribald remarks from a colleague until she squashed him: 'Just because you're on a DSU carrier doesn't mean you have to behave like an animal.'

By a quarter to eight we were in Tottenham High Road. 'Haringey,' said someone, reading from a sign outside Council offices, 'Protecting Jobs Protecting Services.' 'And killing policemen,' he added. It was very strange to watch from a carrier these dull North London streets, the long straight traffic jams between lines of tatty shops of which the very ordinariness had heightened the sinister, thundery impression they had made when the riot was only a quarter of a mile distant.

What you see in a street scene is largely selected from what you expect to see there. (That was one reason for choosing for this book an area of London which had been completely strange to me.) The police see different streets from us at the best of times: most people would not recognise even a burglary in progress should they come across one. This specialised sight of criminality can be quite easily developed by anyone who has business with criminals, but many policemen combine it with a capacity for observation which seems praeternatural when compared with the stolidity and bottom that the job can demand. Driving one evening in an unmarked 'crime car' through the shopping centre of Leytonstone, a WPC pointed out to me a West Indian girl the colour of fudge, wearing a short-sleeved dress: 'See her arms: those bruises. Finger-marks – someone has gripped her by the arm, and on the other side too, poor girl.' We did not stop. Nothing could have been proved.

The policing of a football match is an enormously complex feat of organisation, designed to reduce the unexpected to a minimum, as will emerge. For the most part the police there are not expected to detect anything very subtle going on, but just to stand around and be seen themselves.

The first standing was done in queue for breakfast. This took a long time: there were 600 policemen to feed in a school hall. Nor was anyone in a hurry to get to the food: one rasher of bacon, a small portion of tepid baked beans, and two indescribable sausages, all served on paper plates with plastic knives and forks. I am still not certain whether the liquid we drank was 'tea' or 'coffee'. But we drank a great deal of it, uncertain when next we would be fed.

For most of the serial, such a gathering of policemen from all over London was a social occasion. They would look around for people they had served with or trained with, and point them out to their friends, with brief character sketches. Policemen see their own Force as made up of individuals. This trait would hardly be worth mentioning except that to the outside world it seems that there is nothing behind the uniform. A van full of police in Tottenham: one thinks of an instrument for oppressing blacks, not a collection of young men looking forward to a football game.

Outside, at a quarter to nine, Good Friday held the promise of being a real spring day as we walked through the deserted stadium. The pitch was still almost all green despite a winter's wear; the blue plastic seats in the stands glistened in the sunlight; beneath the east stand was a crowded room with cream breeze-block walls and a nondescript lino floor. All the police officers were uniformed; the walls held maps and a huge duty board saying what each serial would do. The inspectors collected their radios, then were briefed by an eager chief superintendent.

All the police resources were concentrated on keeping the fans segregated; they were to arrive from different tube stations, enter the ground at different gates; and the Arsenal supporters were to be confined to the south end of the ground, with 'sterile' – empty – sections of the terraces, too wide to throw a bottle across, separating them from the home crowd. If arrested, they were to be sent to different stations for charging, according to which club they supported.

The chief superintendent was convinced there would be trouble: he kept saying that intelligence had been coming in all the previous night to the effect that the Arsenal yobbos were planning something. What he was specifically afraid of was infiltration of the north terraces, which would hold Spurs supporters, and where Inspector Thompson's serial was to be stationed. When he called out 'Serial 8', Thompson, whose expression of lazy pleasure as we walked across the ground had been a delight to see, barked 'Sir' as if every line in his face had been ironed that morning along with his uniform.

As we left the room, through a tractor shed now full of police horses, he remarked to me that there were always rumours, and nothing ever came of them. But in the sunlight outside he was once more crisp, briefing his troops:

'Try and identify them: they won't, unfortunately, be wearing Arsenal rosettes. And if they give you the slightest bit of hassle – hoik them out.'

By nine o'clock the serial was split into two groups of ten, each standing in a gangway between the deserted terraces. It was not until 9.40 that the first supporters arrived, for an 11 a.m. kick-off, and began to fill up the Arsenal end, 100 yards from Serial 8. I could, and did, walk around. For the police there was nothing to do but stand and reminisce.

The serial was drawn from ordinary officers, not specially trained, and one of them had been present when the puggy man's daughter was charged. She had already acquired a nickname: Theresa the geezer, since her attitude to the crime was rather different from her father's, and unaffected by either force or authority. She had been surprised that the boy had survived. (By then, it was known that he would.) She was not very bothered either way. Given a chance, she thought she'd probably do it again to somebody; she was, as she freely admitted, in spite of what her father had said, a vicious girl, though fonder of glue than cannabis, of which she rather disapproved. The oddest thing of all was that the boy had been a real friend, and not someone to sleep with. But Theresa the geezer was by then last week's story.

The conversation soon turned to crowd trouble. Units from all over the Met are called to big demonstrations, and many of those present had been to an anti-apartheid do at Trafalgar Square, where they had been pelted with canned sardines and pilchards. No one knew why these had been chosen as missiles on that occasion; everyone knew it hurt like hell to get one in the face.

'And then when Kev punched that guy in the face, and it turned out to be a woman . . . ooh argh . . . She just went straight over backwards . . . But he still swears it was a man.'

After a while, the talk died down. I passed a match programme around. Someone lent me a pair of gloves. Every five minutes someone would remark that there was only an hour and a half, or an hour and a quarter, or some such desert of time, still to cross before the match began.

They could not smoke, and there was some doubt of the propriety of Karen and Michael's accompanying me to the hot-dog stand for something to drink. Once in the dingy concrete bowels of the grandstand they could relax and take their hats off, and chumble at watery sausage, bread like soggy polystyrene, and a hot liquid that tasted of plastic cups. The next chance we got, we drank Coca-Cola.

Out on the terraces again it was curious to stand and be watched by the spectators as if we were as loathsome as the food. We stood between stout iron fences and watched their lumpy faces: as the terrace where there had been fighting the previous year filled, it became apparent that it would be physically impossible to get to a fight there until fear had cleared a space around it. The fixed barriers to segregate the fans were ferociously effective. At the south end, where the Arsenal fans stood, the stand above the terrace was guarded by rotating blades as well as barbed wire. But these precautions also meant that the

42

police would find it as difficult to get into the enclosures as the penned fans would to get out. Someone decided that the only way to deal with trouble would be to climb the fence and then run over the heads and shoulders of the crowd.

But the day was too fine and fresh to worry much about anything except the football. When the match started I moved down to sit with Mr Thompson on a bench beside the corner flag. He had reverted to his manner of feline pleasure, except when Chris Waddle had the ball. 'Complete tosser, with no touch at all.'

Behind us, a middle-aged coloured woman with three children, one white, accompanying her, had seemed a reproach to my distrust of football crowds when she bought peanuts and chattered before the match began. Now her *tricoteuse* voice started hurling advice like broken bottles at the players. 'Break his legs!' 'Kill the bastard!'

The children, too, complained, in quieter voices: 'I came here to see a football match, not the back of a policeman's head.' I slouched lower on the bench, and began to imitate Thompson in the enjoyment of the game. The players, all but Charlie Nicholas, seemed enormous. Their sleek thighs shone in the sunlight; they hurled themselves at one another with great brio and little skill, except when Hoddle had the ball. Though as tall as any man on the pitch, he seemed proportioned like a wishbone: his legs could make a ball do anything, but they could do nothing else. Without the ball, he was an unstrung marionette. He ran clumsily, and instead of jumping, shuffled. He tackled like one of Boadicea's chariots. Mr Thompson thought him wonderful, and I agreed. He was.

Arsenal played better, though, and Thompson's attention was soon distracted to scanning the terraces. Nothing happened there; at half-time we walked through the tractor shed, which now smelt pleasantly of manure from the horses waiting there, and received another gung-ho lecture. The trouble now was meant to take place in a pub after the match: all the serials in the gangways were to take up positions outside ten minutes before the end of play.

'I hope everybody knows what to do, and who to do it to,' announced Thompson when the men gathered round him in the cold at the end of the pitch. The sun had disappeared by now and the day seemed bright only to our eyes, which had become used to the cellar in which we had been briefed. But the crowd remained resolutely peaceful. We came out of the gates just ahead of the first refugees from the game, and took up positions at the head of the road, where it joined the High Road. All the fans passing us should have been Tottenham: all of them should be heading for a quite separate tube station from the Arsenal supporters.

And so we stood. The first outriders of the crowd came running to escape the congestion that would follow; but soon the wide stub road filled up like a river in spate with the contents of the terraces. Few people walked alone: if in couples they held hands, but for the most part came in clumps of five or ten. Few looked at the police, and no one touched them. Karen and four others stood in line at the edge of the pavement, and unless I placed myself in the middle of the line I was constantly jostled. Mr Thompson stood by two mounted policemen on the other side. For perhaps fifteen minutes we just waited while the crowd pushed past, never quite touching, never talking; then he led us up the High Road towards White Hart Lane tube.

Again, the uniform had this faint, but unmistakably repellent effect on the crowd. The effect was entirely different from that produced by a single policeman. Nor did we adopt the ponderous gait, turning only at right angles and always crossing at lights, recommended to

Home Beats. (But, on a small scale, this quick trotting had something of the immunity conveyed in traffic by the lights and siren of an Area Car. Whenever I had been riding in those for a while, I would be astonished when my next lift actually had to stop at traffic lights.)

The drizzle began at the tube station, where there was nothing happening at all, and as we walked back to the van parked behind the stadium the serial itself broke into a straggle of groups. Thompson and a sergeant discussed the case of a CID officer who had come to a sad end after taking an afternoon off-duty to go drinking. I eavesdropped as much as I decently might, and caught for the first time that note of pagan reverence for fate with which those who get caught are remembered.

This is a subject on which it is easy to be misunderstood: an idea exists that the police are merely – or largely, or essentially, some rubbishing word like that – thugs in the service of property. Only the uniform is meant to distinguish them from criminals. This sounds like a left-wing prejudice, but I come across it most frequently in Conservative think-tanks, or among the leader-writers for Conservative papers, perhaps because such people have so little contact with the law.

Probationers learn early: when mock trials are staged at the training centre, an experienced CID man playing the part of a squalid petty criminal will always destroy the police evidence tendered by a probationer. And in any conflict between the law and justice, policemen, being human and full of the knowledge of sorrow, will want to drop the law.

Georges Simenon is quoted as saying once that the message of his books is that there are no criminals, only – perhaps – crimes. The Bill would tell you that there are innumerable criminals, and very few crimes.

Many of the foulest things one sees are scarcely illegal at all: one evening on patrol I met a large Glaswegian, perhaps forty years old, who was muttering about the gas bill while he sat in his mother's front room. It was decorated with the fragile clutter of the old, but bottles lay on the carpet: one still rolling under a coffee table. When she entered the room, the first thing you noticed was how tiny she was; the next, that under her white hair was an enormous bruise around one eye. Two wrinkled ridges of dried blood crossed the bridge of her nose.

But all she wanted the police to do was to throw out her son, not to arrest him. They did this without violence. Legally, and in terms of police procedure, the incident was wholly trivial: 'Suspect left the scene when officers arrived.' Without a complaint, and without evidence, no crime had been committed. It would not have been right to take the suspect outside and beat him up, as some police forces might do, and there was nothing else that could be done. The policemen involved had forgotten the episode a week later. There are so many like it.

This sort of situation, where the law, justice and morality all have opposing and seemingly irreconcilable claims, is very common in police work. And a policeman who cared only for the law could not have the moral standards which the job demands. A policeman who cared only for justice would go mad, while one who cared only for morality might be the maddest and most dangerous of them all. One thinks of the Grand Inquisitor.

'Justice,' said a senior and experienced cop once, 'is when somebody gets his just come-uppance, even when it's for something he didn't do.' More dramatically, an inspector announced one night in a pub that when the Krays ran the East End at least there was fucking justice there: if people did things then, they were punished.

Policing is unusual in that this moral complexity is built into the job even at its lowest levels. In most professions that involve difficult moral choices, the trainee can be shielded: nurses practise 'passive euthanasia', but they do so on the authority of a doctor, and shielded by custom, authority and the impenetrable language of their work. But nineteen- or twenty-year-old constables are confronted with decisions which men of much greater experience would find difficult to make, and which must be made instantly. There is little chance of delegating such responsibility upwards. Senior officers may make some decisions for their men, but there are far more decisions that must be made than there are senior officers.

An inspector beloved by his men once said to me that he would always cover for them: 'If one of my lads got out of line, I'd verbal for him. Give him a bollocking in private, of course, and see he never did it again. But you don't let stuff like that out.'

If the police cannot wholly depend on law, justice or morality to guide them in their work (which also, of course, requires physical courage), what is the code that strengthens them? The great variety of policemen, and the variety of their work, means that the answer itself must vary. But it is all subsumed into the idea of 'professionalism'.

Policing is a true profession in the sense that it is self-administered: certainly, the internal regulations are much more to be feared than the law. But at the moment there is little agreement even within the Force, let alone outside it, as to what 'professionalism' should mean. The old style, based on a judicious mixture of shrewdness, brute force and perjury, has gone for good. What must replace it is as yet uncertain, in part because of the appalling management jargon fashionable among senior officers. They may know what they mean – I believe they do – but their language is almost impenetrable. So the natural sympathy which policemen extend to any colleague who fails at a harrowing and difficult job is added to a suspicion that the rules are being unfairly changed, and slimy politicians are taking over. This is not the same as a tolerance of corruption; it docs mean that men who are for the most part too busy to think about what makes a criminal, and what a crime, have to reflect when another policeman gets caught.

We were saved from more waiting about by our arrival at the carrier. It seemed that the day was over, but as we moved off the radio announced the long-promised trouble at a pub. The serial was at once caught up in sporting excitement. To shouts of 'Let's go' we moved off as rapidly as we could into the fringes of an enormous traffic jam. At first we made good progress, with runners clearing the way ahead, but once we reached the High Road there was no chance of driving at more than five miles an hour. By the time we passed Tottenham nick the alarm had been called off.

With the end of hope and tension, the serial collapsed. Half a mile later, I looked up from my notes to see Thompson's neck stretched out and bobbing gently ahead of me as he dozed. There were only four men left awake in the van.

The next time I saw Mr Thompson, I was running again, this time down Leytonstone High Road, towards the half-used Victorian station there, which is a lot further from the tube than it seems on a map. We had arranged to meet at four and go to Wapping, for the *Times* strike. Just before ten past I reached a coach parked outside the station, waved through the window, and clambered aboard.

This was exceptional work. The twenty-three men on the coach would normally have been the 'late turn' duty at Ilford: the shift, or 'relief', working from two till ten in the evening. The other two reliefs were working twelve-hour shifts to cover for them. This system continued on Wednesdays and Saturdays for most of the spring at Ilford. Thompson's relief expected to work for a minimum of eleven hours, until three in the morning.

The coach was a great deal more comfortable than the carrier had been, not least because the seats were arranged so that four groups of four faced one another across small tables.

We drove first to Greenwich where, in the shield-training centre, an old SEGAS warehouse just east of the Blackwall tunnel, the factory floor had been partitioned off until beneath this noisy high ceiling there was room for several thousand policemen to eat their tea: pork chops in beefy gravy, canned new potatoes and carrots, with apple pie to follow, and the usual indescribably awful coffee. The rule with Met drinks is that if you're not sure what it's meant to be, it's coffee; if it's tea, it's just bad tea.

THREE

'PC Blakelock he is Dead!
Doodah! Doodah!'

It took me some time to comprehend the vastness of this
shield-training centre, which squats like a gigantic brick in
the wasteland upstream of the Thames Barrier. The
weed-fringed concrete slabs that stretch towards the river
are used for practice in hurling wooden bricks. The dining
room is only a partitioned area in the middle of the floor.
Poking around inside on a later visit, I discovered a
plastic-bullet firing range: three concrete walls enclosing
an oblong floor covered in rubble and stacks of tyres; also
two white-painted, converted fire engines, which had
been tested as water cannons. But they take only three
minutes to empty their tanks, and after that are a
defensive liability.

The centre can hold a great many men: we were down
as Serial 950, which would have meant there were 9,000
men there had the serials been numbered all in order with
no gaps. In fact, there seemed to be about 1,000.

There were three types of foot police involved in the
Wapping trouble. The static serials had no riot gear, and
were deployed as the first line of defence. Behind them,
out of sight, waited the shield serials, who were protected
with long Perspex shields – the tops of which were bent
outwards to deflect the flames from petrol bombs –
helmets and flame-resistant overalls. They were not used
until the printers started throwing things, and then their

job was only to hold the line. The arrest squads were equipped with small shields, and still further specialised.

Inspector Thompson came on time to the briefing upstairs, so we had about twenty minutes to kill in the cream whitewashed corridor. There were colour photographs of the shield training on the wall.

Inspector Thompson, stranded by his punctuality, stalked the corridor, and delivered one of the only two racist epithets I heard used in four months. He was showing me the photographs of a huddle of policemen in riot gear, beneath a shower of wooden bricks which other, more animated policemen were hurling from twenty yards away.

'You have to keep moving in a situation. That's what we're taught. But at the Farm the 'groids were up on the walkways, throwing things down at us, which was much more difficult.'

The only other time I heard language of that sort was from a burly off-duty policeman, covered in scratches from a fight he had just had with a black man he had seen stealing car radios in a station car park and chased for 500 yards: 'And then I caught the coon — ' he said. 'Oh you musn't put that in your book.' In both cases, the epithets were provoked by the memory of physical fear. Among younger policemen there is a tendency to use abusive language borrowed from the novels of Joseph Wambaugh – 'The little scrote in the witness box' – but as a sort of private joke and reassurance. If slang is meant to reflect prejudice, then the language of the police reflects a prejudice against all criminals, regardless of race, colour or creed.

There is another objection to the careless use of language: that it offends people. But policemen talking in the canteen are acting just as much, or as little, as they act on the streets. What matters is that their parts should be suited to the action of the play.

There is always a theatrical element in police work, as in any human contact. At Wapping the audience was larger than usual, since newspapers and politics were involved. The demonstrators were as much their own audience as they were participants. People who cared about the dispute behaved as if they could watch themselves becoming better or more valuable as they took up their positions. The senior officers at Wapping directed the demonstrators in one obvious sense: they might walk here: they might not cross there. But they were also directing the performance of their men, and very conscious of this.

After we had waited twenty minutes in the corridor, and prowled into the briefing room, there to read the standing orders on riot alerts and posters from the RUC in Lisburn on how to search for arms and how to check your car inconspicuously for booby-traps (the explosive must be precisely placed if it is to kill the driver, which makes it slightly easier to find than it might otherwise be), Chief Superintendent Rowe arrived and summoned the inspectors and sergeants of the other serials from their meals to be briefed.

Mr Rowe worked from Leman Street police station, which covers the area. As is usual, each serial was given a briefing sheet stating their duties, and stating, too, the ten standing orders, which laid down the procedures for everything from co-operating with the press to charging those arrested.

The CS impressed three things on the officers: the importance of good relations with the residents, whose concerns he was most worried about; the importance of good relations with the television cameras: 'You are to tell your men that we have nothing to be ashamed of: I don't want to see any hands going over TV lenses when I watch this on the news'; and the success of the operation so far:

'Five hundred arrests, and not a single case dismissed.

We've had lots of bindovers, but not a single case dismissed. This operation has been conducted with a high degree of professionalism so far, and I am proud of it. . . . We must keep the standards up.'

I was to hear this briefing several times. The guts of it always remained the same; but later jokes crept in, like the one about the woman who the National Council for Civil Liberties had claimed was personally insulted on thirty something separate occasions by policemen trying to keep her from her home in Wapping. 'Would you make it quite clear to your men,' said Mr Rowe, 'that they are not to ask for identification from people who say they are residents, and that way she might meet at least one policeman who doesn't insult her.'

But what struck me on that first briefing was that the men were expressly prohibited under all circumstances from entering the News International plant except through the front gate, because it was impossible to cross the barbed wire even if the fence went down; and anyone trapped there would have been a stranded target, and very probably seriously injured before he could be cut free.

Nothing much happened on that first visit. We got lost, of course, heading for the rendezvous, and then there was a mix-up about shields. There were an insufficient number on the bus: Inspector Thompson sent two men out to walk half a mile in the rain to collect the remainder. The rest settled down to do nothing for a while. The coach, which had smelt strongly of farts as we left the scene of our encounter with Met catering, ceased slowly to do so. Some people settled to murmurous card games round the tables in the back.

There was less ribaldry in the quiet conversations than I had expected. Someone complained about his Walkman: 'When [the tape] hits the bottom, it comes off.' 'So does my missus!' . . . (and looking up at me with a quick guilty

53

laugh): 'in fact I'm thinking of getting a mirror on the ceiling to watch her . . . '

Yet most of these young men, along with their money, had acquired considerable responsibilities in their private lives. A favourite topic of conversation was the purchase of houses; another, the birth of children. In the front, Thompson and his elderly, burly sergeant talked about Tolkien; Rachel read a book about pot plants. One reason, perhaps, why the *bien-pensants* despise the police is simply snobbery. Looking around the coach I realised that there was not one activity or converstion being pursued that *Private Eye* would not have found intrinsically ludicrous: Tolkien spoofs, gadgetry and pot plants are the staples of the false Christmas ads which fill the centre of the magazine once a year; and *Private Eye* is probably the most important disseminater of opinions (as opposed – God save the mark – to information) in the country.

The commanding officer that night was CI Vick, who was regarded by Thompson's serial as an eccentric, because he seemed completely unauthoritarian. The sergeant had earlier explained that Mr Vick would actually apologise if he gave you a bollocking but found out afterwards that he'd been wrong to do so. It was not the courtesy which seemed remarkable, but the idea that a senior officer might admit that he had ever been wrong. While we waited for the men to return who had been detailed to fetch the riot shields, he swung open the door and looked in. Thompson explained about the shortage of equipment. Mr Vick was unemphatically angry: the equipment should have been on the bus; if it were not, it should have been collected as quickly as possible, not at the pace of walking men.

'Suppose trouble were to start while they're collecting it?'

There didn't seem to be any likelihood of that in his

judgement, replied Thompson, who believes that senior policemen are 'officers', not 'management', as the Yard would have them known. He retained a feline confidence in his own authority: since the route that the two men had taken could not be known, he could not be ordered to go out in the coach to look for them. Besides, one could tell that he thought that the arbitrary nature of authority was essential to its successful exercise. The rain outside was disagreeable: hence it was an excellent idea to send men out there briefly.

After Mr Vick had left, a system was arranged whereby four men and a sergeant were sent off to watch the top of the road, but quite clearly nothing was happening. The demonstrators were a thin, dispirited shuffle.

At around ten the boxes of snacks with which we had been issued at the training school were broken out, and with them the high spirits of the young men. Oranges hurtled up and down the coach, unaimed; then the brown sauce packets started to fly, and for a while the interior seemed as if a blizzard had hit it. But there was no lasting mess, no ill-humour, and nothing else to do.

Up at the junction with The Highway, the main road on which the demonstrators passed, Mr Vick was waiting. He greeted me by name. There had been quite a lot of fuss made about my accompanying the serial off their ground into H District; a fluttering among the press officers, who were used to having journalists confined to one spot and eager to impress on me how dangerous things might become. But Mr Vick was not surprised that permission had eventually been granted. The Force had stopped pretending that all of their 27,000 officers were good, he said: they had also come to realise that most were good. 'That inspector you're with seems rather stupid,' he added.

He asked what I had learnt: I said the most important

55

thing had been to realise that I would have to answer one question for every one I asked. He seemed to think this shrewd – policemen expect very little from the press – and went on to bitch quietly about the Murdoch executives who thought that their money allowed them to dictate police tactics. This didn't bother him much: it was just another rather saddening example of the greedy stupidity of the world. For thoughtful policemen it must be a relief to enter middle age.

When next I returned to Wapping with another group some weeks later the weather was better. The dispute had grown older and more bitter. It was even then, at eighty-nine days, the longest-running public order problem in the history of the Met. Mr Rowe could no longer boast at his briefings that no one arrested had got off; for the serial I came with, from Barkingside, duty at Wapping had become part of the routine of police work just as the Home Beats from east London had found themselves patrolling Broadwater Farm for most of the winter.

When we arrived at Greenwich, there was a drill in forming 'belt cordons', where you grip the belt of the man to your left with your left hand, keeping the right free for defensive purposes: this is an improvement on the old technique of forming a cordon in which each man had both arms linked with his neighbours'.

But the rehearsal was perfunctory and not wholly successful: shouts of laughter as the line wheeled and collided with itself. Later I heard a story of a similar rehearsal in a camp for the miners' strike, in which two serials were pitted against each other, and the incident ended with two inspectors rolling around and fighting on the ground. There was not much to do for the first part of the evening but talk on the coach, which this time was parked east of the plant and north of The Highway, by a junction where the demonstrators were to be stopped from passing further and blocking the main route out for the lorries.

We had been told at the briefing to expect about 3,000 demonstrators, far more than had come the previous weekend, when, Mr Rowe explained, 'the extreme Left had been off dealing with the Libyan crisis'. This time, they would be back in force.

> They're the people who will stand at the back or in the middle and push and shove and wind up and shout. They'll throw marbles or pennies, or if we're very lucky, 10ps . . . There was a bottle full of an inflammable liquid, fortunately not petrol, thrown at a TNT lorry in the Commercial Road last week; I want the lads to be aware of that danger.
>
> . . . and the picket have started taking the numbers of particular policemen before they start abusing them for three or four hours until the guy cracks; then they make a complaint. If any of you see that happening, I want you to take the guy out of the line at once.

But numbers were to be worn, even with overalls, so as to make complaints possible.

From seven to nine there was nothing to do in the coach; the streets were still light; the weather warm. The coach door was open, but few people left; one man read a textbook on psychology; some gossiped; at the front, the inspector and his sergeants reminisced about the miners' strike – known as 'The mines'.

Conversation had three topics: drink, food and fighting. All were treated in unexpected ways. The fight they remembered was between the two inspectors who had got carried away at a rehearsal. The men on the coach felt far more sympathy for the miners than they did for the printers, and there were no memories of picket-line

57

fighting. For the most part, they were proudest of the way in which some – striking – miners had come to see that they were not the monsters of left-wing demonology. In fact they had given much of their surplus food to miners' families. When the catering works, policemen are amply fed: some of the DSU carriers are said to hand out food to the tramps on the Embankment.

I suspect that the evil reputation of the Met outside London arises less, in fact, from left-wing propaganda than from the rivalry between different police forces. Just as Essex is known as 'Bandit Country' to Met policemen driving home, who will tell you that the Essex force has a prize pot which goes every month to the first man to bust a London policeman for a traffic offence, and just as each happy section of the Force believes all others are incompetents by comparison, so must the county forces spread the legend of the Big Bad Met.

At last word reached us that the march was on its way. Mr Rowe had said at the briefing that he expected 3,000 demonstrators: I was never able to work out whether the consistent over-estimation of the numbers expected was the result of faulty intelligence, or an attempt to make the troops feel that their battle was important. So often, as on the first time I went there, nothing much happened at Wapping. This evening, the internal estimate was of 1,800 marchers, and something rather nasty did happen.

There was another serial parked ahead of us: their inspector had a faulty radio. So when the order came to deploy along the north side of The Highway, and to cut off the side street at Cannon Street Road, Mr Sanger's serial was out first, and had already chosen the fortified half of the position before someone went to tell the other serial where it should be.

Sanger's men were lined up on the grass in front of a council estate, with a waist-high iron fence in front of them. Eastwards, and to our left, the other serial covered the mouth of the road itself, between the high spiked railings around a churchyard and the low fence protecting the green.

The marchers came on slowly: I slipped through the cordon and went down to join them as they approached the gateway to the Murdoch plant. At the head of the procession came Mr Rowe, walking backwards. Behind him, the SOGAT float, with a huge poster of a pathetic child weeping because 'My Daddy helped Murdoch make millions'. There was not, as one might have expected, a further float from the NGA saying 'Murdoch helped my Daddy make millions' behind that, but two men in long Indian headdresses, with cream-coloured trains of feathers waving and nodding down their backs, who were beating a large drum held between them by a crop-haired woman.

The drum had not the funereal, shuffling tempo of the marchers, who were confined by the float to whatever speed CS Rowe found himself comfortably able to walk backwards. The drummers beat out to the cheery rhythm of a football chant: 'Hate the boys! Hate the boys! Hate the boys!' Some people heard 'Paper boys!'

At each repetition of the slogan, the marchers behind pointed their fingers towards the clumps of police behind crash barriers who were guarding the south side of the road, where side streets led down towards the NI plant. One man gave the words through a megaphone. All this hostility was curiously undirected at the actual policemen who walked on the north side of the procession, mingling with the marchers every five yards.

The march was terribly slow and casual: people kept weaving in and out on to the pavement on the north side, which was neutral territory, at least until we came to the stretch held by Mr Sanger's serial. As they approached this, I nipped ahead, and slid through the cordon.

The sky was fully dark now; the road clearly lit by

59

yellow sodium lights, which gleamed brightly from the helmets of the mounted police, who had formed a cordon across The Highway about 100 yards beyond Mr Sanger's serial to block off the pickets from Wapping Lane, where the distribution lorries would emerge.

The chanting faltered and became subdued. One of the stewards took a megaphone with which to address Mr Rowe, fifteen yards in front of him. He asked whether the marchers would be allowed to continue, 'because if you don't that proves you're totally on the side of the bosses'.

This rather Reaganite, megaphone diplomacy had no effect. The procession moved confusedly to the stub-end of The Highway between the main cordon and the serial next to us, which blocked the way northwards up Cannon Street Road. This serial was grotesquely outnumbered, but the twenty men still had not linked their belts, partly because they were wearing macintoshes, as earlier ordered, which made their belts difficult of access. So they formed an informal cordon, squeezing more closely together. Two of the demonstrators tried to squeeze their banner past: the first one got through, but the second of the pair was sent back and his partner followed.

From the crowd came a confused and raucous roaring: 'Scaaabs', then a thin voice from a megaphone announced that they were going northwards: 'Just follow the banners!'

These had retreated slightly from the waiting police, so that there was a space of about six feet in front of the belt cordon which now hurriedly formed, each man fumbling with his neighbours. Sanger's twenty men kept their position on the higher grass behind the railing, covering a frontage about three times as long as the twenty men on the road below them, whose formation seemed ludicrously fragile in the face of a crowd of 1,800.

The crowd became noisier and more excited, full of collisions like a heated gas; then a whistle shrilled above the confused roaring and twenty to thirty burly men started running through at the cordon, which recoiled five or ten yards at the shock, then snapped about two-thirds of the way along. The men on our side scrambled up against the railings and stood there unmolested, though anyone who'd fallen would have been badly trampled.

The crowd, the banners, everyone, followed this charge around fifty yards up Cannon Street Road, past the police coaches for about fifty yards. Some climbed the railings and started to run down the grass. Every second man in Sanger's serial had been sent to run after them as the cordon broke: Sanger himself started to run down there, and as we approached a scuffle moved towards us on the grass: two men walked clumsily towards us, as if disagreeing in a three-legged race. One was a stocky, bearded PC, the other a little dark-haired man with blood running down each side of his eye, away into the sideburns on one side, and down the side of his nose to the corner of his mouth. The blood seemed black in the street lighting; his face beneath it yellowy white.

Alongside these two came a burly, tall half-caste with a long Tibetan scarf hanging down, and a bespectacled, fiftyish man wearing the tabard of a march steward. The steward was seething with Hampstead indignation as we arrived. He claimed that the wounded man had been hit on the ground. 'Outrageous', he kept saying. Beyond him, the marchers who had broken through the cordon were still heading in loose groups towards the undefended northern end of the street. The situation seemed beyond tactical control, for once the marchers gained the cross-street at the far end, they could infiltrate east and down to The Highway where the lorries were to leave.

Sanger lost his temper for a moment, and snapped at the bespectacled steward for 'making a political remark'. This sidetracked the conversation for a while, since he had then to deny repeatedly that he had said any such thing. Then the steward remembered his main business, and demanded that the bearded PC be arrested for assault. Sanger explained he could not do that: he had come to take a complaint. The steward grew angrier:

'Yes, complaints! Police investigating police! Why can't we arrest him? Do you want the two of us to go and do a citizen's arrest like we tried last week? Then we just get arrested. Why can't we have the same rights as you?'

This went on for some time, while a hostile group gathered round the fringes of the argument: at last Sanger suggested that the bespectacled man try and get a summons from the magistrate, which shut him up. Names and addresses were taken: the tall half-caste claimed to be 'David Braithwaite of the *Guardian*'; the bespectacled man was a solicitor. Further gouts of indignation were released when he was asked for his work extension: he was a partner; he did not need an extension number.

All this took around five minutes: up at the far end of the street a cordon had formed as we arrived, and the wounded man was being tended by a pretty young WPC beside a traffic police Rover, outside a pub. A group of young men and women watched, and passed loud remarks to one another about poor blokes who get beaten up on the ground – the speed of rumour is astonishing. The bullish, bearded policeman, who was in ordinary uniform, and turned out to be a Home Beat, whose usual duties were to plod round streets and schools being an ambassador for his Force, leant against the car, silent and ill at ease.

The man who claimed to be from the *Guardian* was taking down numbers and addresses. He wanted to know how to make a complaint about his jacket, which had been ripped in the original struggle. He started to complain about the length of time which the ambulance was taking to arrive: at last it appeared, just behind a coach full of policemen in full riot gear. The wounded man was helped aboard and 'Braithwaite' went off muttering. 'This will make a great story.'

The shield serial had not disembarked from its coach: the pickets who had come up the road marched down to The Highway again, singing as they went to the tune of 'The Camptown Races': 'PC Blakelock, he is dead! Doodah! Doodah! PC Blakelock he is dead, doodah, doodah, day!'

For a while things were calm after that. Back at The Highway, Sanger's serial reformed its line, and the men talked in low voices about hitting people. Unlike Mr Thompson's men, they were not a shift drawn from a single police station, but an *ad hoc* gathering from all over the district. No one knew well the man who had lashed out: they too were certain that he had 'sticked the bloke on the ground'. A gaunt Irish PC had heard the truncheon strike: he said that whatever the provocation had been it was quite out of order to hit someone as was done. Since truncheons are rounded, and designed to break the skin, it was necessary to be especially careful to use them only on arms and legs, as you are meant to. About half the serial had not even bothered to bring their truncheons with them: the Irishman said he had only used his once in fifteen years. Even in baton charges, he said, the idea was only to canter, not to run, so that the crowd in front of you had time to get out of the way.

Even Mr Sanger had only used his truncheon once:

'I was chasing this bloke once – disqualified driver – and I caught him. Then he escaped, so I ran after him again and we fought and he got away: I was left holding his jacket. And I had pulled my truncheon out to say: stop this or you'll get hurt: I was holding my truncheon in one hand and his jacket in the other; and he was running away. There didn't seem anything to do but to hit him over the back of the head so I did. And I tell you one thing, Andrew – he ran a damn sight harder after I done

63

that than before . . . coloured bloke he was, too. And when I think of it, it was just stupid.'

Some time later, at lunch in the senior officers' canteen at Barkingside, the subject came up again, when cricket was exhausted. Sanger repeated his belief that truncheons were unnecessary. He stretched out a beefy arm, corrugated with muscle, and studied his large, irregular knuckles: 'Yes, if you've got to hit somebody, just punch them. Broke my hand on one bloke once . . . '

Does this sound violent? There are policemen who get pleasure out of fighting: a very different pleasure than one might derive from simply beating people up. A fight, in this sense, has rules – about which weapons may be used, for instance – and winning within these rules has a value which winning at all costs could not have.

Those rules correspond roughly to a pre-existent working-class morality shared by police and public alike in east London: it is that order from which Londoners deviate when they are 'out of order'. This code was never wholly binding; nor should it be sentimentalised. The Kray twins, in their career as amateur boxers, might have seemed to subscribe to it: but in their parallel and simultaneous career as gangsters the key to their success was that they admitted no limits to violence, eventually murdering a prisoner whom they had themselves encouraged to escape simply because he was getting inconvenient. And the Krays, it is worth remembering, flourished unhindered by the police in the early 1960s, though everyone knew who they were, and what sort of things they were doing. To say that is not to argue that the police were inefficient, or corrupt, but that their efficiency depends in the last resort on a superiority of force. What protected the Krays was the silence of witnesses, glamourised as the East End code: the code was broken only when potential witnesses believed that the law was more powerful than the gangs and could protect them.

But though the old rules were insufficient, they were not valueless. They did have a certain civilising effect, since they contained a rather Aristotelian concept of the just use of force. This force could on occasion be considerable: the most violent story I came upon while with the police was that of an old man who made the mistake of interfering with the daughter of a Greek family: relatives found him in his car, pushed a shotgun down his trousers, and fired, half castrating him.

The punishment had here a certain relation to the crime involved. But the characteristic of modern violence is that no such relationship can be discerned.

The pre-moral, and in the Greek sense barbarian, character of the modern hooligan is best illustrated by a story which has no violence in it at all:

I have an Aristotelian friend named Mark, whose extravagant and fairly illegal young manhood has left him unscarred but for four dots tattooed on his knuckles, a sign that means 'All coppers are bastards'. He now programmes computers, and wished, one night while I was writing this book, to entertain his wild young brother up from the country, Oliver: I brought my girlfriend, who edits her parish magazine. The entertainment was to be provided by Nick, a Mancunian in his early twenties. He had been living with his Dutch girlfriend for the last year or so, but it was not for this that one remembered his views on women: once he pointed at a girl about ten feet away and said fervently to me in his normal voice 'I'd like that sitting on my face and saying "I love you".' Irony was to him a form of insult: he once beat up an Irish youth quite badly for being clever. Mark, who is larger, had pulled him off his victim, and reckoned that otherwise he would have put the Irishman in hospital. So it was a surprise to find Nick's girlfriend with him in the pub. She was looking calm and happy. He said they'd got engaged that morning. He'd even bought her a ring.

The celebrations continued through several pubs, each noisier than the one before. The fiancée drank apple juice: as Nick became louder, she quietened and shrank until her cheeks seemed fit only to make cider from.

Young Oliver rose splendidly to the occasion, telling stories of wild pubs in Hertfordshire where the catch-phrase was 'Out in the car park' [to fight], and where one man roamed the public bar on Saturday nights with his dork hanging out of the front of his trousers. Another man, whose girlfriend was offended by the sight, remonstrated: 'What's the matter?' said the bemused exhibitionist, 'I didn't dunk it in your beer, did I?'

These stories culminated in an account of an unfortunate young man striving to overcome the disadvantage of a middle-class background who had been fired with the lust for glory one evening, left his friends, and gone to the roughest pub in town. He had pushed open the door like John Wayne and swayed there for a moment. Then he had leant more comfortably against the doorpost and unclipped a screwdriver from his belt.

'Right!' he shouted, 'EVERYBODY out in the car park.' The noise gradually subsided until the whole pub was staring at him in silent awe.

'Come on you bastards – are you afraid, or what? Out in the car park! . . . And I don't want any of this crap about one at a time either. I want all of you at once.'

An hour later, his friends, among them Oliver, realised where he'd gone and set off to find him.

We looked all round the car park, under the cars and everything. But we couldn't find him anywhere. So at last we opened the door and asked if this crazed bloke with a screwdriver had been in.

'Friend of yours, is he?', they asked.

'Yeah', we said, getting ready to run.

'Oh, he was a great laugh. We brought him in and gave him a drink!'

Now this was clearly meant to be a story of heroic braggadaccio, with well-understood conventions, but Nick was deeply affected: 'The man's crazy – I mean a screwdriver! You can't do anything with a fucking screwdriver! I mean if he'd had a Stanley, he could have got four or five of them. But a fucking screwdriver!'

His voice, full of drunken earnestness, cut through the noise of the pub like a rivet being dragged over rusty iron. He repeated his encomium to Stanley knives several times, then decided he wanted to go to this pub sometime. 'Would I be safe there? I mean, I don't mind a good smacking, but I don't want to be smacked.'

We moved on. In the next pub he sat across the table with Oliver and Mark, while my girlfriend sat between me and the fiancée, with whom she tried to talk.

He started to boast: he was a despatch rider, a fucking good despatch rider. He meant, he made £300 a week, clear, he wasn't joking, like. (It was in fact true that he had been a despatch rider until he tried to ride 500 yards home after a pub crawl and shot a red light in front of a police car.) He warmed to this idea of his riches, and elaborated it for some time, pausing only to demand cigarettes from the other men present every five minutes. After he'd told my girlfriend that the ring he'd bought his fiancée had cost £2,000 that morning, an idea, or something quite like one, occurred to him. He leant over to me.

'Andrew, d'you mind if I ask you a personal question? I'm not trying to be funny, like. I'm not trying to be funny, but d'you mind if I ask you a personal question? Now, I'm not trying to be funny, but have you ever, like thought of getting married?'

Without pause for thought I answered with complete dishonesty.

He continued to boast about his money for a while, then he leant over to me again, and confidential as a foghorn, asked if I minded if he asked a personal question.

'I mean, this is a really personal question, Andrew. I'm not sure if I ought to ask it, like I mean you don't mind, do you? I'm not trying to be funny, but it's a really personal question. In fact, it's so personal that I think I'll ask Mark if I ought to ask you. I'm not trying to be funny, but it's a really personal question.'

He rose unsteadily to his feet. Mark stooped towards him: through the noise of the pub I heard again Nick's raucous confidential blare: 'Is he fucking that, or what? Can I move in there?'

Mark gravely advised against asking this question directly – or at all. My girlfriend, talking to the fiancée on her right, heard nothing. The reason for delicacy, as Nick had seen it, was that his fiancée might have overheard the tender question if he had put it directly across the table.

None of these people has much time for the police. All of them might at some stage of their lives have been considered habitual criminals: one had even been a social worker. Yet Mark and Oliver could be wholly trusted. I wouldn't like, as a policeman, to have to deal with either of them; but it could be done, and both sides would understand what victory or defeat entailed. There couldn't be any rules when dealing with Nick, since he has so limited a conception of the self to be ruled. He's not a psychopath, however violent he may be from time to time: he's honest with money, and has a genuine sense of fun. But he cannot imagine any social unit larger or more demanding than a group of mates, any more than he can suppose that women (who are always 'it' or 'that', never 'she' or 'her') belong to quite the same species as he does. He is pre-moral, not even amoral, and he is the wave of the future.

FOUR

The Cuirassiers of the Frontier

To police the dispute at Wapping was a political act. That's not how the police themselves thought of it: certainly it made little difference from the ordinary run of police work that the people being coerced on this occasion thought what they were doing was justified. Even the common burglar is untroubled by qualms of conscience: he must be, since they are the only serious obstacle you must break down before you break into a normal house.

What made the dispute at Wapping political were actions outside the control of the police. If the Labour Party had been in power, the law would not have been the same and the problems might have been quite different ones. The Government might have been prepared to see the mob break into the plant, in order peacefully to persuade their brothers to stop working. This would still have been a breach of the peace, deprecated by all men of goodwill, and possibly fatal for anyone who got caught between the mob and the wire. But it would have happened, and afterwards the defeated would just have had to try and be understanding.

Neutrality was impossible in such a dispute. The police did not feel themselves to be on Mr Murdoch's side. They tried to take the side of the residents of the neighbouring council blocks, and of any other neutrals who might be found. But this could not keep them above the fight, nor make them enjoy it.

Chasing criminals is what they joined to do. You can't

be neutral there either, but you know you are in the right. This attitude expresses the profoundly activist, extrovert character of the job. 'You're not a policeman in an office: you're a policeman on the streets,' as the proverb in the ranks has it; and most policemen would say with Marx – if the source of the quotation was unknown – that the philosophers until now have tried to understand the world. The point, however, is to change it. I think that the attitude is best expressed in a poem by Robert Graves, written for the barbarian auxiliaries of the later Roman Empire, 'The Cuirassiers of the Frontier':

Goths, Vandals, Huns, Isaurian mountaineers,
Made Roman by our Roman sacrament,
We can know little (as we care little)
Of the Metropolis: her candled churches,
Her white-gowned pederastic senators,
The cut-throat factions of her Hippodrome,
The eunuchs of her draped saloons.

Here is the frontier, here our camp and place –
Beans for the pot, fodder for horses
And Roman arms. Enough. He who among us
At full gallop, the bowstring to his ear,
Lets drive his heavy arrows, to sink
Stinging through Persian corslets damascened,
Then follows with the lance – he has our love.

The Christ bade Holy Peter sheathe his sword,
Being outnumbered by the Temple guard
And this was prudence, the cause not yet lost
While Peter might persuade the crowd to rescue.
Peter renegued, breaking his sacrament.
With us, the penalty is death by stoning,
Not to be made a bishop.

> In Peter's Church there is no faith nor truth,
> Nor justice anywhere in palace or court.
> That we continue watchful on the rampart
> Concerns no priest. A gaping silken dragon,
> Puffed by the wind, suffices us for God.
> We, not the City, are the Empire's soul:
> A rotten tree lives only in its rind.

The police are meant to detect criminals from known crimes. This is at least what they pretend to do, and what, very occasionally, they succeed in doing. In fact the effort is only usually made for major crimes, and is not always necessary even then. 'If a murder takes more than three days, then you know it's going to be a sticker,' said a man who spent nine months on a murder investigation. But for the most part the police are trying to identify crimes from a knowledge of criminals. Murder is a special case in that the possible suspects are then identified by opportunity or motive rather than habits of life. But if you get a robbery or a sex-crime or practically anything but a parking offence or a burglary – both of which, it sometimes seems, are committed by everyone who has time on his hands – the first thing to do is to check out the usual suspects. And if there is no list of usual suspects, do nothing.

The system for deciding when to act and when not to varies from station to station. At Ilford these things are not centrally decided. Crimes are passed to various 'squads' as they come in, and these squads decide, for the most part, what will be done.

The 'Beat Crimes' squad thinks of itself as the cream of the station. The poor Burglary squad has quarters even more cramped than theirs, and crimes even more thankless; the District Intelligence and Information Unit, whose job is to predict crime in useful ways, has for obvious reason even less success; but the Beat Crimes squad, when not dealing with piddling autocrimes, gets the thugs.

The hours are extremely long: the pay, in consequence, very good. David Price, the sergeant in charge, reckons he makes about £19,000 a year, counting overtime, in his early thirties. And he loves the job. One night he rang me at home, at seven, to ask if I wanted to arrest someone, and did I mind waking up early?

At 6.30 the next morning I reached the station with burning feet, lungs full of ash, and eyes that had apparently been varnished open.

Some of the others in the room were hardly in better case. Price himself would look chirpy and freshly showered if newly arrived in Hell, but his taller subordinate Kevin Garner, heavy-set and balding, looked as if the inside of his skull had been sandblasted.

The squad sat at their desks or leant against the walls. We drank sticky black Nescafé while Price perched on his desk with his feet on a chair and the papers in the case beside him:

'Shall I tell you the story? We've got this robbery reported in Leytonstone on February 9 . . . A woman who works at the jeweller's going to the bank with £1,400 in cash and £4,500 in cheques. She's knocked down and robbed. There is a witness who saw an IC1 and a Turkish looking bloke and chased them to their car.

'Our info is that it was set up by a girl who works in another branch of the jeweller's: Maggie Timbs. She went sick that day. Her boyfriend is Greek, and we think he's the one that done it. The van they used was seen later dumped on the street where she lives.'

The squad divided: the two weightlifters, blonde, rangy Gordon Main, and black Richard Pile, who were teased round the office as 'Schwarze and the Negger', went off in one car to arrest Maggie, along with Karen Gilmour. I climbed into a pale blue Ford with Price and Garner.

Ilford in the dawn was not unlovely. It is far enough from the East End proper to be prosperous by British standards. The new yellow shops could be worse; the streets are tidy; the cars one sees, clean. We headed away from the centre (shoplifting, fraud, assault) through quiet residential streets (burglary, domestic disputes, murder). Everything seemed decent, peaceful and asleep. We saw only two other cars, a milk-float, and a newspaper boy.

Price explained more to me: 'The ID evidence is not much good. We really need to find a bit of a cheque or something, to pin it on him.'

We drove down a street broader and more suburban than the ones before. I remarked on this prosperity, and was told the houses were worth an easy £80,000 each. Then we pulled up, and waited for a moment, examining the house diagonally opposite. There seemed nothing to be gained by waiting; it was just a moment of regretful consideration.

Garner locked all the car doors carefully while Price walked up the drive, muttering to himself the difficult name of the man they had come to arrest. It was five to seven exactly, Price rang the bell.

Just as we began to get impatient, waiting in the porch, a face peered from the upstairs window when Garner walked up the short drive. He flashed his warrant card upwards, in a gesture almost like a wave.

A jingle of keys approached from inside; a slumping but still handsome grizzled man of about five foot six opened the door.

'Mr —?' said Price, holding his warrant and card in front of him. 'We have a warrant to search these premises investigating a robbery.'

The grizzled man, moving heavily, showed us to his son's room. We filed up the stairs of the quiet respectable house and opened the door to a medium-sized bedroom. Rambo sat slouching on the double bed, dressed in a pink tank top and white long johns. Above the bed hung a faded Chelsea scarf; the floor was dominated by a weightlifting bench; two large barbells lay on the carpet. Down one wall was a long white wardrobe with a vanity table built-in: a mirror surrounded by two shelves of cosmetics.

Price showed Rambo the warrant, then laid it, with his radio, on the television set.

They started to search without fuss, checking through piles of clothing and envelopes. Extraordinary, the things people keep in their wardrobes. Rambo had bundles and bundles of letters from girls.

Price is small and chirpy and polite: Garner pale, heavy and polite. No one listening to them work would suppose that Price was the superior officer: he seems so light on his feet that gravity sits badly on him. No doubt this illusion comes in handy.

'What do people call you, mate?' he asked.

'Rambo,' with a look of some pride.

'Don't want to insult you by getting the name wrong.'

That was in fact the name their informant had given them, and they searched for a while with renewed hope.

For the moment, Rambo sat patiently on his bed. He said as little as possible; and while he could keep his hands steady when his wrists rested on his knees, they kept coming back to his mouth. He pulled his underlip and examined a flake of skin with the gravity of an extremely vain young man (the walls were decorated only with weightlifting posters of the body beautiful) then went back to pulling the outside of his overlip. But as the search continued and nothing was found, he gained some assurance, and began to look as if his sulkiness mattered.

He moved to the weightlifting bench while they searched under the mattress. They found a bundle of dole forms there: Rambo was evasive about where he worked and how he afforded his frequent visits to the Hippodrome, loquacious about a visit undertaken to California the previous autumn. There was also a report from a hospital.

'How d'you get that?' asked Price.

'Fighting down the Kings.'

'Uhuh. D'you win or lose?' sounding interested.

'Neither,' with a sheepish grin.

Later they told me that he'd been smashed over the eye with a beer glass: 'Yeah. Glassed down the Kings: an occupational hazard.'

Dim sounds could be heard from the rest of the house. Once I looked down to the edge of the door beside me, and saw the mother's eyes, which had the sheen of black olives, looking at her son.

'Shall we do the shed?'

Garner shook his head:

'We'll pull him in. I'm arresting you.'

'You can't. Show me your warrant.'

'Don't need no warrant.'

'I know my rights. I'm going to ring my solicitor.'

'No you're not.'

'You can't arrest me.'

'I just did.'

'I know my rights.'

'You can ring your solicitor from the station. Not from here.'

'I'm going to ring him. You want to stop me?'

'Look,' said Price, 'either you come with us now, or we get a couple of cars and there's a lot of fuss.'

Rambo rounded on me: 'What are you doing? Am I being shown, or what?'

There was a pause. The presence of two policemen in the room was not as reassuring as it might have been. Neither was nearly the size of Rambo, and both were behind him. I was not. But he turned abruptly, and went into the bathroom. Tremendous sloshing and garglings: Price went to the television, picked up his radio and called two cars.

Rambo emerged, and began to pick his clothes for jail.

He put on first a shocking-pink blouse, then thought, and changed to a subdued red and salmon checked shirt.

He announced again, that he was going to ring his solicitor. Just then the reinforcements arrived, led by a large uniformed man with a moustache. We all trotted down the stairs. No hand had been laid on anyone. At the bottom, Rambo turned down the corridor into the kitchen, and Price followed him. There was another altercation about the solicitor: one could hear only Rambo's voice:

'Fuck off! Cunt! Just fuck off!'

Then his father's voice, full of hoarse outrage:

'Don't you be rude to policemen.'

They all emerged, moving in line towards the door, Rambo calling his solicitor's number over his shoulder; the father turned back, and suddenly it was all over. I found myself standing three feet behind the others in an open doorway, looking down the corridor that stretched empty and defenceless against the morning. It was just gone 7.15. There was no doorknob, so I pulled the door shut with its knocker and hurried to the car. We rode back to the station in silence. The worst part of the day was now over for us; for Rambo, in the back with David Price, the bad part was about to begin; on the streets that we rode through the day hadn't started at all.

As soon as Rambo had been parked in the cells, the canteen seemed full of policemen, though in fact it was only the six members of the Beat Crimes squad getting their breakfast after two hours' work. Garner fell on the video machine, stabbing the 'fire' and 'bomb' buttons continuously with two stubby fingers. The party who went off to arrest Maggie told their story:

'The mother opens the door, and we say who we are, and can we come in – and she says it's not a convenient time. Not a convenient time!'

It seemed a wonderful message from the world out

77

there, where people still can have convenient lives.

'I thought you were going to get clumped for a moment there,' David Price told me.

'I thought I was, too.'

But the arrests had passed off peacefully, and the conversation soon turned to more interesting matters. There is something – I am not sure what – about police canteens which makes people think of food. Richard Pile, the black plain-clothes man, was joshed for eating a toasted Mars Bar sandwich at work once.

After half an hour the work resumed. Maggie was talking freely about uninteresting things. The first name she gave for Rambo's friend turned out to be inaccurate; but she was taken out in a car and pointed out the house where he lived. Five minutes with the phone book turned up what seemed to be the right name; an expedition found his sister; she said he was working at a bank in the West End; another expedition departed.

I was not welcome, as they were going to talk to the manager first. David Price, at this stage uncertain whether this was the man they wanted, said that it was an example of the way in which they mess up people's lives: the 'Not convenient' rerun for real.

'The bloke will probably have his career wrecked whatever happens, just from the embarassment of being arrested in the office. Ideally, we'd wait until he comes home, but there just isn't time, and we have to consider the victim's rights as well.'

Richard Pile and I were sent off to get a warrant to search the suspect's home. He was relaxed and confident, a young man at ease with his ambition.

The magistrates' court is a neo-brutalist bunker in two storeys. It is doubly pleasant inside because you can't there see the outside. I had plenty of time to brood on such matters while Richard typed up the warrant forms: this was my introduction to CID typing: which is done with the index finger of the right hand, very slowly, and with frequent mistakes.

The courtroom had a Scandinavian air of panelled decorum without ceremony. Three magistrates were sitting: two sharp middle-aged women, and an older rather dissipated-looking man, who said nothing at all. Richard, who had been lounging so confidently outside, and who walks with the bounce of an athlete, was quite transformed at the witness stand. It is a sort of lectern: he held it with both hands, and rocked as he spoke in jerky and tentative sentences. The magistrates talked across one another, largely for Richard's benefit; and quickly agreed to the warrant.

Leaving the court, once more bouncy, he said with relief that such experiences were exactly like being up in front of the headmaster.

'But this is a middle-class area. They really hate robbery and residential burglary. They'll give you anything for that. Sometimes I have to tell them the ins and outs of a duck's arse before they'll do it . . . but sometimes they're quite OK.'

In fact the magistrates' court at Wanstead is much more popular than the court which serves Leytonstone, which is derisively known as 'Disneyland', or 'The Fun Palace'. The police are by their nature activist: they're not thoughtless, and some are given to reflection, but the end of thought is for them action, not contemplation. Further, they believe that jailing criminals is a morally good thing to do; and that almost everyone charged is guilty.

'The law is an elaborate game. Justice is when someone gets his just come-uppance, even when it's for something he didn't do.' That remark first heard on a rather drunken Friday evening when an old policeman was explaining himself to me, kept returning to me throughout my time with the police.

The contempt and distrust in which 'working' policemen

hold the apparatus of the law can hardly be exaggerated. It can, however, to an extent be understood: when I first came to Ilford, I was shown around by Inspector Dick Slater, a young man from Derbyshire who had something of Brian Clough's marked resemblance to an angry hedgehog. He was not in fact nearly as young as he looked; nor was he in the least bit stupid, and I regret our subsequent quarrel. His apparent youth, and our quarrel, were caused by the simplicity of his beliefs. Duty to him seemed as self-evident as the requirements of punctuality and obedience: after I sat up till three one night typing up preliminary notes for this chapter, and slept through a subsequent appointment with him and others the next morning, he was able neither to forgive nor to understand my behaviour.

But before this, I had taken him to lunch in a pub and he recounted there a conversation he'd had with a friend of his, a magistrate. She had remarked that she never sent anyone to prison unless she had to, because she believed that English prisons are so barbaric that the crime which would deserve such punishment – let's have no cant about 'reformation' in Pentonville – is almost inconceivable. I have a lot of sympathy with this idea, and said so. He thought it treachery against decency and good order, which are not trivial things: and as a policeman, he knew what happens when decency fails.

'Suppose,' he said, 'that I were to attack you with an axe. D'you think that would be attempted murder? No: you or I might think that any reasonable man who swings an axe at another man's head must realise there is a risk of killing him, and is prepared to take that risk, and should be held responsible for his actions. But in court he'd say he didn't know what came over him, of course he never wanted to kill his friend . . . We'd be lucky to send him down for GBH. He wouldn't get two years.'

Lest this seem exaggeration, it is worth remembering

that one of the Brinks-Mat bullion gang was able to stab to death a plain-clothes constable whom he found creeping through his garden, plead that he had been terrified by the sight, and be acquitted of murder and manslaughter alike. The murder of PC Blakelock was horrifying enough, but dreadful things have always happened in riots. That is why they are justly feared. It is the apparent welcome given to Blakelock's murder by Bernie Grant, and still more the jury's acquittal of the man who killed PC Fordham, which indicate a far more serious rupture in the necessary structure of society.

Writing that, I remember that I am never certain what 'society' means in practice. It is a word I distrust, and use as little as possible in an attempt to write clearly with words I can understand. Policemen have few such inhibitions, because they are empiricists. 'Society' means to them the totality of police and public: they are a part of it at the same time as they defend it. Nothing in this book should be misunderstood to suggest that the police feel themselves outside society, or beyond justice. But that is not enough to make them love, or even trust, the apparatus of the law.

'D'you know what the acquittal rate at Snaresbrook Crown Court is? Sixty per cent. And you see, Andrew,' said Dick Slater, 'I know that 90 per cent of the criminals tried in the crown court are guilty. Mind you, I'm not saying that the other 10 per cent were innocent: just that I don't know for a fact that they were guilty.'

This was not really a grumble about the leniency of the courts, but a plea that his special knowledge be recognised. Dick Slater is in his late thirties, and rose, therefore, through an honest Force. Policemen now in their fifties will reminisce about the old ways of getting round a court, which were simply organised perjury: a chief inspector – not to be more closely identified – once

spent the fag-end of a Friday afternoon drinking whisky
with me in his office:

'The best used toilet in the Metropolitan police is up at
— Crown Court. Two minutes before they're due on the
stand, everybody's in there.

'And d'you know why? It's because they're offering
their career. I mean, when those young men get up on the
stand, 97 to 98 per cent of what they say is going to be
absolute factual truth – but there's always a little bit that
isn't. And that's what's worrying them. There's always
something you have to change in order to fit the legal
definition of a crime. And it worries everybody. It worries
me. You get those experienced men from the CID, and
they say it doesn't worry them; you look at their faces,
and you see nothing. But I watch them, and two minutes
before they're due to witness, they're off to the pisshole
too.'

'Has this got worse since you started?'

'No, no, it's got very much better . . . the law's better.
You see, Andrew, when I started, you had to tell maybe
70, 75 per cent truth in the court, and the rest was . . . '
He gestured with his hands like a man manipulating a
steering wheel. 'But the Theft Act 1968 made it much
easier to catch burglars. Before then it was so difficult to
get the legal bits complete. Now there's only a little bit
you need to get right.

'Drunken driving, too. Before 1967, you virtually had
to prove that the man was incapable of getting into the
car. So if he wobbled when he walked, you said that he
staggered; if he staggered, you said that he was falling
over; if he fell over, you said that he couldn't stand up.
After 1967, it was dead simple: you just took a little blood
and a little breath, and that was all you needed . . . '

Another policeman of the old school, also reminiscing
over whisky, described being sent out as a trainee with an
experienced Home Beat: 'You'd get put on traffic stops,

and he'd say: "Do that car" – and the light would have to be fucking red in court, no matter what colour it was . . . it was dreadful, but you learnt.'

While on the subject of veracity, I should point out that these conversations are reconstructed from notes made immediately afterwards. I would happily swear, though, that they are accurate in essentials, and especially in the crucial phrases.

There are more interesting things to be said about the attitudes here revealed. The first is that the police would not regard it as corrupt to lie in court in order to establish something which they know to be true: whether they'd think it right, or even politic, would be another question. The answer – I would guess – would vary from case to case. Corruption would be to lie when you did not know; or, worse, to lie as a result of some inducement; or to plant evidence, which is something different again.

The second is that I know no one outside the Force who believes that the police do habitually tell the truth in court. I had not supposed they did when I started this book, though I now believe they do, and that this represents a reformation that has gone largely unnoticed, especially among magistrates.

Experience of two related things has caused me to change my mind. The first is the high value that the police put on honesty outside court. I had expected to be treated courteously, and I was. What I had not expected, but found to be true, was that the occasional discourtesies I bumped into were the result of plain speaking, and as such a necessary preliminary to good relations. It is easy to see why the police should put such a high value on honesty among friends: the most obvious reason is that almost everyone they deal with tells lies. The exercise of power is fundamental to police work, whether this power be naked or clothed in authority and custom. To understand power you must read Machiavelli; there you find that:

> One can make this generalisation about men: they are ungrateful, fickle, liars, and deceivers, they shun danger and are greedy for profit; while you treat them well, they are yours. They would shed their blood for you, risk their property, their lives, and their children, so long, as I have said above, as danger is remote; but when you are in danger they turn against you . . . Men worry less about doing an injury to one who is loved than to one who makes himself feared. The bond of love is one which men, wretched creatures that they are, break when it is to their advantage to do so; but fear is strengthened by a dread of punishment which is always effective.

Such a view of the world is exhausting to sustain clearly; but it is what you see from behind the charge-room desk. It is not all of life nor even all of police work, but to have seen it at all makes essential the preservation of some oasis of honesty at least. It is hard enough to be an honest policeman; it would be almost unendurable to be a crooked one.

And the more that people lie to you, the more you must practise discrimination of the truth from lies; which requires that you recognise and use the truth yourself. The great difference between a policeman massaging his evidence in court and the criminal doing the same is that the policeman knows what he is doing. (It is not worth trying to nail in this way a man who can afford a good lawyer.) I think this is a moral distinction, rather than the result of an adversarial system of justice: a friend of mine who was researching a television programme about criminals in Sweden, where the system is inquisitorial, found a prisoner who claimed he had been fitted up. The interview with this man lasted four hours, while he listed every iniquity of the judge, the prosecutor, and the investigating officers. So eloquent was he that in the end, drained by the effort of constructing his proof, and overawed by the result, he said, with the shock of intellectual discovery – 'You know, I might just as well have been innocent.'

The second, and related, reason why I believe policemen have become more honest in court is that the reasons they gave for lying were always tactical: they lied in order to make the real crime they had detected fit the legal definition of a crime. When the legal definition of a crime is changed, they tell the truth. It is better policy, apart from anything else. It is difficult to appreciate this point without realising how artificial is legally admissible evidence; but they learn that in training, as will be shown later.

There is for the police a fundamental distinction between information – which is what they believe – and evidence, which is what they hope the courts will believe. Information is almost always what the courts would call hearsay, since there are only two ways of acquiring it: either someone tells you what he's been doing, or he tells you what someone else has been doing.

This attitude need not imply the use of paid informants. They certainly exist, but are only really used for larger crimes. It does, however, imply that suspected criminals are arrested before one is certain what they have done. To quote a senior officer again:

> The vast majority of detected crimes come from arresting someone. Quite often you arrest somebody and you're not quite sure what they've done. But in the process of discussion and interrogation, it all becomes clear. If we were up a level, say at I&SU, or C11 [the central anti-gang squad], then it wouldn't

work quite like that: the really big league criminal, that's a bit different. Then you target them first, and try to find out what they're doing and with whom before you arrest them.

But 75 per cent of detected crimes come from arrests, at least in this division, and this kind of policing is what policing's about.

But on the day we arrested Rambo I had not yet realised the special value of information, and committed a frightful solecism at what seemed to be a moment of triumph. Around noon, a phone call came through from the policemen who had been despatched to Oxford Street. They had successfully arrested their man; he fitted the description given by a witness to the robbery who had seen one robber taking off his balaclava in the van used to escape; and he had taken the day in question off work. That seemed to clinch everything.

Dick Slater then asked me how things were going: I told him the story thus far, and added, in David Price's hearing, that I supposed the original tip-off, naming Rambo and Maggie Timbs, had come from a disgruntled girl of Rambo's. This guess represented no great feat of deduction: who else would have turned him in? But it must have been true, for Sergeant Price spurned me ever after. I had exposed his information, and therefore his power.

But information is useless if it cannot be used to extract more information. Throughout the afternoon Rambo and his friend denied everything. Maggie talked freely, but hardly about interesting things. The squad grew more and more frustrated. Maggie was the first to be released. David Price had tried everything he could think of:

'Last thing I did, I told her he was shagging the world – shagging the fucking world!'

Not even this appeal to treachery worked.

Rambo's solicitor arrived at last, and after all the fuss

was liked by the police, since he too reckoned that his client was guilty:

'Even his brief says he's a lying shit – and I'm quoting!'

There was, however, no proof, and nothing to be done except to organise an ID parade at some time in the future. In the meantime, the yobs were released (and never, so far as I know, charged). The formalities took until eight in the evening; the last thing I saw was Kevin Garner kicking a piece of office furniture in a rage, not as a substitute for kicking a prisoner, but because he had around midday become convinced that these were the men who had knocked an old woman to the ground and stolen her employer's cash, and he simply could not prove it to any black-gowned judge.

FIVE

Shabby Equipment

Assume, for the moment, a policeman whose favourite poets are Eliot and Graves. The Met is such a large and diverse force there must be four or five such people among its 27,000 officers. This man might claim that the cuirassiers of the frontier are altogether too romantic. His *esprit de corps* might even lead him to deny that Geordies, Scotsmen, and the Welsh can properly be compared to Goths, Vandals and Huns. The more serious objection is that the cuirassiers have a life far more simple and further removed from the white-gowned pederastic senators than the police can enjoy. A much closer analogy to the confusions and inadequacies of police work then appears to come from 'East Coker' in *Four Quartets*:

> . . . And so each venture
> Is a new beginning, a raid on the inarticulate
> With shabby equipment always deteriorating
> In the general mess of imprecision of feeling,
> Undisciplined squads of emotion. And what there is
>   to conquer
> By strength and submission, has already been
>   discovered . . .
> There is only the fight to recover what has been lost
> And found and lost again and again: and now, under
>   conditions
> That seem unpropitious.

Out in Woodford one has time to reflect on these matters. This is a new station beyond the North Circular Road, between two duckponds and the golf-course. As in most police stations far out from centre, security is tight. They probably have fewer visitors in a week than Ilford has in a day. But doors are locked with numbered combinations, and these combinations work.

The Child Care squad, two and a half people housed in a spacious room with yellow pastel walls, the board above the desks that are pushed together covered in cheerful photos of policemen with children in clippings from the local papers, wives and children in little snapshots, four 35mm prints showing the duckpond through the four seasons. Behind the door is another bulletin board, that can only be seen from inside the room. There are professional quality colour prints with a velvety sheen to them: an arm the colour of pork crackling, and broken up in much the same way by a panful of boiling water; a pair of buttocks gouged and lacerated, with their two thin legs faintly bruised; a pale torso faintly mottled with bruises the grey of a school uniform sweater.

Some of these wounded bodies have faces attached. An Asian boy lies across a hospital couch with his arm stretched towards the camera, unable to believe it can hurt so much. A blonde and blue-eyed girl looks into the camera with nothing apparently wrong with her except an expression of overwhelming defiance and pain. A baby has – not a *black* eye – but a bright blue crescent bruise alongside her nose.

'Oh, no: these aren't the worst. We put these up to show people how to look for small things. That baby had six broken ribs when we examined her, and it was all spotted from one black eye . . . Children have pliable bones – you see, we pick up the jargon – but there are some injuries that can't be self-inflicted. A torsion fracture, for example: when you pick up a baby by the ankle and the leg twists, now that can't be self-inflicted. And if you get two black eyes without a broken nose as well, then that's two separate injuries: it's always two separate injuries.'

Jean Crawley, who told me this, is a leonine blonde with an oval jawline and interested green eyes. Her manner is collected, for like most police officers she is most shocked by crimes which are outwardly unspectacular:

'There was a case we had which was just three burns across each hand – not a serious injury, really. But the father had heated an electric soldering iron first and put it across the boy's hands to stop him from stealing . . . 90 per cent of what we get is just over-chastisement. What cannot be condoned is the use of instruments.'

I asked which instruments.

'Boiling water, whips, horse-crops, rolling pins, cigarettes . . . fires . . . for someone to think that they have to boil up a pan of water or put the kettle on, and then walk over to the child and pour it on them: To my mind, that's barbaric.'

Any assault on a child goes to a detective chief inspector, because it's always a major crime. Whenever possible they send a police photographer to the hospital, though they have on occasion used a pediatric pathologist.

A weighty man entered the room: about six foot tall with brown hair, brown eyes, and pale skin, like chamois leather. A seam like a scar ran across his forehead when he raised his eyebrows.

'I want to rape a woman or something. It's been a bad day.'

'You've just missed the coffee, too.' said Jean. He settled heavily, and almost without pause began to talk to me with measured anger:

'Sometimes I think that either we're insane here, or the agencies are: I've just had a twelve-year old girl who wants to be a model, so a photographer comes round to do a portfolio of her. And when they have finished the usual pictures, he says he wants some glamour poses; and the mother allows it. They take shots of her topless, bottomless, in suspenders and a garter belt and so on. Twelve years old!

'And the social services say, yes, they think someone needs help in that situation . . . No way do you let a twelve-year-old girl pose for indecent photographs! My own girl is fourteen and I wouldn't let anyone outside the family take a photograph of her at all . . . The mother thought it was quite all right – the girl wants to be a model, and she's prepared to do anything to make her rich and famous. And the father leaves all that sort of decision to her . . . Yes, it is illegal, I checked, Protection of Children Act 1978, Section 37.

'The trouble is that if we take the child into care, she will feel that she is the guilty one, since she has been punished, by being removed. I don't know what to do with cases like that. It's very difficult to imagine how parents can do things like that.

'This year the sexual abuse figures have gone through the roof: Woodford and Chingford we call 'perversion valley', there's so much of it about. What sort? Well this year it's ranged all the way from rape and buggery over eight years – starting when the girls were six – down to a mother masturbating her four-year-old girl at a nursery school, in front of witnesses . . . The father in that family is a sex offender; and the eldest son, well, there's a court case pending about him . . . The mother just has no idea of what is permissible or not.

'The national average for the prosecution of all child abuse cases is about 2 per cent. Round here we prosecute about 10 per cent of the cases; normally only for the serious offences: a broken bone, an open wound, or serious sexual assault. The majority are convicted.

'From our point of view, those are almost the easiest to

deal with, in a way. The dilemma in smaller cases is whether to take the children into care. In this area, we try to make a joint decision with the social services and other agencies, though both sides have unilateral powers, which they use. Our role in this office is basically to be a buffer between the CID and the social services, and there's a natural mistrust on both sides. But we get some good information from the social services.'

Then he went home to his wife. I sat in the canteen, staffed by drab-coloured, raucous women with bad teeth, and wondered which of the trainees I knew would discover how little there is to conquer.

For Woodford is also a training station. The probationers of J District come there at regular intervals to be taught more than they have learnt at Hendon. They come in very much as cuirassiers, or hunters; their teachers are older, more reflective men, who would understand the *Four Quartets* – trappers, rather than hunters. They have had at least fifteen years' experience of the inadequacy of all human justice; while training on the streets teaches probationers confidence, the classroom training can at least teach them the inadequacy of the law.

This comes as a continual shock to the young cuirassiers. Eleven of them, ten men and a woman, were gathered in a room for a course on 'Courts and Presentation'. This seemed to make little sense at a time when the Crown Prosecution Service was about to take over almost all the responsibilities of working policemen in courts, changing all procedures; but the need to give evidence in contested cases would still remain. This is thought much harder in magistrates' courts than in crown courts. In the discussion preceding the rôle-play, one young man complained that he hated Waltham Forest Court, where 'There's some scrote in the dock, and he's guilty, but they're treating me like dirt.'

This cracked the class up. Some of the cleverer ones

looked at me sideways to see if I were writing down the word borrowed from the police novels of Joseph Wambaugh.

The earnest tall young man, fitted with difficulty behind his desk, was offended: 'I don't mean contested cases. I mean where he's put his hands up to it and everything.'

It's a nice point whether the young policemen are more shocked to discover that everybody tells lies to them, or to discover that everybody nowadays supposes that the police lie in court. The older ones may be amused by this, as they remember the Golden Age when policemen were believed, and could tell lies effectively.

The instructor told a story from his own days as a probationer, of a sergeant who had said to him that 'We're our own worst enemies': 'He meant that if we didn't tell porky pies, there wouldn't be a problem. The conviction rate would go down to about 1 per cent, and then we might get sensible laws for a change.'

Then he swung the discussion round to the general problem of making evidence credible. This is by no means as easy as it may seem, when the rules of evidence are as tight as they must be. To tell a damning true story is to use hearsay, which is inadmissible. You cannot say, for example, that 'Mr Cox told me Mrs Cox was hysterical, and chasing Mr Knox round the kitchen with a corkscrew in her hand.'

You must say that Mr Cox approached you, and in the light of what he said, you went to the kitchen where you saw . . .

The trouble with this rule is that we interpret what we see in the light of what we expect to see, and of what we have seen before. The first step in telling a story is to decide what it is. If a policeman believes that the story he sees is that of a thief, he will in the first place see the suspect's behaviour as thievish – and this sight of the matter need involve no conscious distortion at all. Even if the English system of justice were inquisitorial, rather than adversarial, the police would still believe that they caught criminals whom the courts let off.

The lesson was driven home for the probationers with a little playlet, in which one of the probationers had to play the part of the prosecuting policeman, Another was the magistrate. One instructor was the clerk of the court – a more important part, the other was the defendant: both played their parts with immense relish. The plot or background to the playlet was that the defendant was a petty thief who had been invited to do an odd job, and then helped himself to a tape recorder in the householder's kitchen, which he had later been seen selling down the boozer. The police had statements from the aggrieved householder, from the man who had bought the tape recorder and from the defendant.

The case could not have been more clear-cut. But the prosecuting policeman was almost as nervous as if it had been the real thing. Thin-voiced and tentative, he looked up after every sentence to see how the clerk of the court was taking it. While he gave his evidence and outlined the case, one had time to appreciate the afternoon sunlight which never seems lovelier than in a schoolroom. Then the defendant took the stage. Though the statements had described him as five foot eight inches slim, and with cropped hair, he was in fact balding, tall, and with room for about three thin men to struggle freely to get out from inside him. He assumed a confident Glaswegian whine, and with an appallingly realistic mixture of truculence and self-pity dominated the courtroom. In about five minutes he had wrecked the prosecution's evidence; the clerk of the court told the magistrate to dismiss the case because of the element of reasonable doubt, and all was over.

The purpose of this training was not to instil in the probationers a distrust of the courts. That is something the hunters seem to put on with their uniforms; and the instructors put some of their best efforts into making their charges reflect on the reasons why courts and the whole awkward civilian world are as they are. The young cuirassiers, after all, need hardly have experienced ordinary life before they are made responsible policemen. They certainly need never have earned their livings at anything else. But it is necessary for the instructors to show that they themselves understand what 'working policemen' feel if they are to get their message across, 'The Christ bade Peter sheathe his sword, and that was prudence': the cuirassiers had to be shown that there were prudential reasons for occasionally sheathing swords.

The subject came up most clearly in a discussion of Broadwater Farm. Someone asked first why, when the Commissioner had promised that it would never happen again, the police now found themselves once more completely passive at Wapping. Then someone else asked why baton rounds had not been used at Tottenham. They were not primarily grumbling, as older policemen might have done: they genuinely wanted to know – at least until the instructor asked them what they thought the pressures on a senior officer 'in a riot situation' were.

Four or five voices suggested at once that the desire for promotion was all that actuated the management. No one suggested anything else out loud.

'With us, the penalty is death by stoning, not to be made a Bishop.' The instructor worked his way carefully towards a fresh idea, keeping as closely to cover as he could:

'To be honest, I felt like most of you . . . I personally think that baton rounds could have been used . . . Any senior officer worth his salt should have given the order . . . But I don't know if that's the answer.'

At last, one of the older recruits, a man who read the *Guardian*, pointed out that the police are almost completely dependent on public opinion anyway. He was later advised very strongly to go for promotion, as were three others in the group. Perhaps they were not real cuirassiers at all. But then it is very difficult to be sure that *any* police officers are quite as out of touch as it is the fashion among the ranks to believe that all the superior officers are. Even those most convinced that 'There is only the fight to recover what has been lost, and found and lost again and again . . . under conditions that seem unpropitious' learnt of it as cuirassiers.

There is a very serious difficulty of police management here. One of the remedies most often suggested by outsiders for the problems of the police is to restore some form of graduate intake. 'If only they were properly officered,' goes the argument, with its unspoken premise that most senior policemen now are too stupid for their jobs. Unless one makes the blanket assertion that all senior policemen, or most of them, are stupid enough to be unfit for any reasonable job, this can only mean that intelligence is more important among senior policemen (who have to deal with respectable middle-class opinion) than among the juniors, who have most to do with criminals.

This argument will clearly appeal to authoritarian policemen, if recast in the form 'If only the PCs would do exactly as they're told then we wouldn't get these messes (and if only the public would do the same)'. But excessive authoritarianism is functionally indistinguishable from stupidity, in as much as it involves a refusal to learn from the messy world. No conceivable set of rules or orders could prepare anyone for the varied emergencies of even one night in an Area Car, or one shift in the charge-room. One could on this basis construct a very persuasive case for a promotion policy which would forbid anyone of outstanding intelligence to rise above the rank of inspector – and quite a lot of policemen would argue that this has always been Force policy.

The instructors themselves exhibited all the skills that

cannot be taught in police training. They all had at least twenty years' experience before joining the training branch. Between them, they had worked in practically every branch of the Force. Two were sergeants, one an inspector: all constituted excellent arguments against promoting intelligent officers automatically.

The Met is constantly training people in one way or another. There are courses to fit people for the jobs they already do, as these change: training in the use of riot gear; training in the vagaries of the PACE. There are special two-week courses for constables on the beat, which one of the instructors described as 'a sort of retreat, really', in which they are encouraged to allow their feelings to show. To be a good cuirassier is not enough to live by, especially as police work on the streets is much more solitary than most jobs. It is only members of the squads who can derive constant strength or comfort from one another's presence: such classically unglamorous and vital police jobs as breaking the news of a death take a lot out of the people who must do them, especially if they joined to nick villains. Hence the endless fund of jokes on the subject. A rather stolid, Dixonian Home Beat officer once told me that he was tempted, when breaking such news, to say, 'Yeah, I got some bad news for you. Your old man's stretched out in a plastic bag on the M1.'

Then there are courses for promotion. After two years' service you can apply to take the examination, though a chief superintendent must issue a certificate saying you are competent to do the job. That is not, of course, enough. There is a central annual exam covering law and procedure in January each year, for which classes start in May the preceding year. At first there is only one and a half hours' voluntary tuition each week; as the exam approaches, the amount of time spent studying runs up to two or three hours a day; when the exam comes at last it is strictly competitive: there is a minimum mark, but if more than the planned intake pass, only the top 140 or so are 'made up' to sergeant.

There is an alternative procedure to allow experienced constables in through interviews and selection boards, even if they have not done too well in the examination. After four years as a sergeant, another round of exams and recommendations raises candidates to the rank of inspector. The teaching for these exams moves to the next level of complexity: not so much how to deal with the people in front of you as how to make things look right for people who aren't there. The list of steps which must be gone through before an inspector can raid a house in an 'ethnically sensitive area', according to one examination paper I saw, would take the best part of twenty-four hours to carry out. The inspectors also get 'authority training' in classroom role-play. Above that level, all promotion is by boards of three men who are helped by the yearly assessments from the candidate's superior officers.

This system, with its blend of formal and unquantifiable qualifications, is interesting as being law that the police have made for themselves, as opposed to the laws which other people make, at which they constantly grumble. For the most part they are happy with it. Certainly, the earlier stages of the process are not resented by the unpromoted. Nor does one hear inspectors grumbling about what happens above them. Yet the fact remains that the lower ranks have a pagan, Kiplingesque attitude to 'the powers that be'. Your own chief superintendent may be a known 'guvnor', whose character can be assessed. Beyond him rises a different order of creation, one not necessarily superior to the cuirassiers. A sergeant working 'on the streets', put it clearly one evening when he was rather drunk:

'That midget Newman, that idiot we call Commissioner, this twat talks in telephone numbers, in language we don't understand.'

The Commissioner's offence was to attempt to please politicians, and especially politicians thought anti-police, like the Shadow Home Secretary: 'Kaufman is a slimy, no-good fucking shit: that snotrag! that dirty snivelling fucking snotrag. Come on Andrew. Write that down!' And there it stands in my notebook – and a lot more. I never heard any policeman swear like that at, or even in the presence of the public.

But the same man, later on in the party, in the same mood of anguished denunciation, told someone that 'what you've got to remember is that policing as we fucking knew it is dead and gone.' The whole training system of the Met may be seen as an attempt to deal with this problem. The fat volumes of police general orders, known as 'all our mistakes since 1829', can only show that this problem is not a new one.

The training policemen have a different perspective. Sergeant Morrisson has twenty-two years' experience. He sat in the District Training Unit office, a narrow room with a dull brown felt carpet, lined with shelves and folders and files. There were even two filing cabinets, one of which held an electric kettle stamped 'MP', teacups and so on. He did not think there was all that much that the training branch could achieve on its own:

'I should really be a salesman to the street duty' [who look after the probationers at work]. Most of what they have to learn should happen out on the streets.

The new style of training is full of acronyms and elaborate jargon which, unwrapped, turn out to conceal simple, difficult things. 'Human awareness training', also known as 'policing skills' is explained by Sergeant Morrisson as meaning 'We try to teach them what makes people tick; and what makes policemen tick.' Even the hated PACE means only, the recruits are told, that they should treat the public as they should like to be treated themselves.

'Human awareness training' is officially anti-racist. It means not the sort of human sympathy which is needed to – say – break the news of a dead son to a mother but the realisation that Asians and West Indians are human too. A lot of this has been forced on the police by the need to look good to the outside world: quite a lot more by the demands of 'professionalism'. In other words, some of it has been produced because the police need to seem to be doing something about riots, and some of it because they really need to prevent riots.

There is a vague idea around that more black police would help to prevent riots, because they could be used to patrol black areas. Nothing could be less attractive to the black police themselves: they joined as policemen, not as racial policemen. There is also the objection that the black criminal or rioting classes are much more hostile to black policemen than to the white. The Asian PC who patrolled Broadwater Farm before the riots was personally threatened with death as 'a traitor to his race' (and kept on that patrol afterwards despite his sergeant's interceding for him).

It is as difficult for an outsider to realise why the police behave and talk as they do as it is for a policeman – frightened, angry, and tired, perhaps – to judge the effect he is having on a group of people he would never meet outside the job. And since so much of police work is devoted to dealing with the unmentionable, the only form of bullshit popular in the Force is authoritarian bullshit, which makes them appear stronger. Nor is even this universally popular.

Sergeant Morrisson again: 'The Police Force is trying to launder people now, and make them seem whiter than white. But I think it was worse to be a woman in the early years than it ever was to be black. In those days you were either a slag or a stuck-up cow. There was a bloke named Ward twenty years ago. He was the chief instructor at

Peel House, and he'd walk into class and say, "Get your tits off the desk". Women now benefit from positive discrimination. There was a period when that happened, though no one would admit to it. And in my view positive discrimination is the only way to get police from ethnic minorities. I don't say it's right: I think it's wrong. But I think it's the only way.'

I have two ways of telling a young policeman in plain clothes. One is by looking at his hands. The police are the only occupational group who dress and behave like members of the prosperous middle classes, yet keep the huge hands of labourers: not chapped or calloused, but unmistakably enlarged by exercise. The second is that they can say, 'I don't think it's right: I think it's wrong. But it's the only way to do it.' That is a style of thought inseparable from a job that requires you to sink down into the slime, embrace the butcher, and yet be aware of what you are doing. Rules cannot be laid down for this style of thought, since it is both moral and pragmatic. That doesn't stop rules being laid down, either morally or pragmatically, nor does it mean that these inadequate rules need not be taught. But it does mean that they will always be inadequate; and that what makes a man suitable as a police instructor are those skills which he cannot transmit.

This came out clearly when the instructors were discussing their charges, with the help of dossiers on which everything, even the 'confidential' essays they had written about themselves at Hendon, was recorded:

'I think that on the streets he'd have trouble keeping his head above water.'

'I'll tell him that without doing his kneecaps in.'

'But I think he's done just enough here. We'll have to keep an eye out for him when he comes back.'

'Talk to his supervising officer.'

After class the trainees were taken, one by one, to a

more comfortable office than the DTUs, where they were shown their reports and asked to sign them. They could write comments, too, but seldom did. The qualities demanded here were not those of a cuirassier, especially when they were asked to comment themselves.

First, a confident young man, who had done well. He leant one elbow on the desk as he read, then asked on what basis the judgment had been made. 'B is unacceptable to me: not in terms of what I'd done, but in terms of what I demand from myself.'

The next one was, the instructor had decided, a 'kick up the arse job.' Inspector Poulter was brisk as the boy marched in:

'Have a read of that, and then have a read of what I have to say.'

The boy slumped with his arms folded, gripping each other, and with rounded shoulders. At the end, he looked up, hoping it was over, and asked only, 'Where do I sign, sir?'

Poulter showed him, then asked: 'Do you think you should take this lying down?'

The boy gave the sort of smile that it hurts your chest to make: 'Well, after I finished street duties with a bad report, I fell apart.' He still looked puzzled, and Poulter switched almost at once into an exhorting encouraging manner:

'You've got to force yourself into as much learning experience as possible. Try and be a bit more clued up, you know. Try and learn some common sense – and despite what people say, you can learn common sense.'

'Working' policemen, as the cuirassiers call themselves, are very often fit, which helps them work their long hours; but even the unfit ones have the sort of clear eyes which good health gives people. Their purpose is simple, and can be accomplished. Like the innocent's in the *I Ching*, the hunter's misfortunes 'come from without': when he fails, he does so because society is not arranged as a hunting park. But the reflective, trapping policeman is not so protected.

Superintendent Terry Cross would be in his early fifties. He looks like a man who broods on things that can't be changed, but he was dressed much more smartly: a purple cord shirt with a white collar; beige check trousers, polished fawn shoes, a blue and red striped silk tie.

Above this, his face was a map of stress, worn with long fingering. There were patches of red veins like blood-worms in front of his ears; his black eyebrows seemed almost worn away; there were little grey rims round the greeny-brown iris of his eyes.

Mr Cross had the quietest voice of any senior police-man I met. He leant back in his office chair, and seemed to be talking to himself. It was only after half an hour that my first impression of a cosy and comfortable office wore off, and I stopped to notice the enormous steel filing cupboard – much bigger than a mere cabinet – that covered one wall.

'The police,' he said, 'have two functions. I call them the symbolic and the pragmatic; and the odd thing is that people outside worry more about the failures of the symbolic functions. The pragmatic, at least here in J outer, is hardly a problem.'

From Woodford it is only a short drive to Norman Tebbit's constituency of Chingford. There is far more to burgle in this belt of London than down in Ilford or Wanstead, but there are fewer burglaries, and violence outside the home is almost unknown. Here as every-where, a uniform means largely what those who do not wear it want it to mean, but what they want here is reassurance rather than active protection.

Mr Cross is the Community Liaison Officer, which means that he is really the Force's ambassador to any group that feels itself to be a community. Like a real ambassador's, his job requires him to be intelligent and act stupid. One thinks of CLOs as dealing exclusively with anti-police groups: in fact the communities on his patch are thoroughly respectable. Woodford and Wanstead have the largest Jewish communities in Western Europe; the Asians of Waltham Forest are respectable professionals. The progress of a prospering gangster, from Plaistow through Wanstead, to Chingford, the Essex Coast, and finally exile represents the path of increasing prosperity for legitimate traders, too.

One of Mr Cross's responsibilities is to the Youth Section, where police authority is almost wholly symbolic. There is nothing that can be done to children below the age of ten; between the ages of ten and seventeen, policy in the Met is closely regulated by the Home Office. Policy may have changed by the time this book appears, but I doubt it, since it is formed less by the amount of crime than by the resources available.

The rule in spring 1986 was that court appearances were only considered after the third offence. Nor do the local police have much say in deciding which children should be charged. The Youth and Community section at Woodford gets dossiers on every single case. This adds up to an enormous amount of paper. One afternoon in Ilford, three Asian boys in their early teens were brought into the charge-room by a store detective. The parents of one had been away for the weekend, and he had helped the others to steal a couple of track-suit bottoms. It was about as trivial as a crime could be. The desk sergeant knew perfectly well that nothing would come of it, and the children were released after an hour. I saw their dossiers when they had reached the Beat Crime squad on their way to Woodford: there were seventeen bits of paper per child.

The most frightening things of all are not even illegal. One evening in the charge room at Ilford at around eight fifteen, there were two immensely fat boys of ten and six, and a third, thinner one, who looked about eight, with an oval face and eyes in which life occasionally flickered. They had been found sniffing glue in the railway cutting of the Essex to Liverpool Street line. The fat boy's mother was almost spherically symmetrical. Her skin was pale, the colour of dirty oatmeal; she was short as well as immense. She suffered from a sort of lisp which she countered by making a bubbling sibilant at the back of her palate. The noise was so awful that after a while the desk officer started to imitate her unconsciously, as one limps when walking with an injured friend. She blamed the thin boy: her son, she said, had given up sniffing glue before.

'We had a male nurse down to stop him,' she said. It sounded as if she'd had him touched with a relic, or called in a witchdoctor. That ended her responsibilities. It was the greatest power she seemed able to imagine.

Her son sat like a golem. Occasionally he whined or looked sly, but one had the impression that he was merely imitating what he had seen other children do. There was no accusation in his shallow eyes. The young fat brother still seemed a child as he looked admiringly at the older boys. The charging sergeant advised 'remedial treatment at home'. The mother told them they'd never sit down again.

I don't think that case ever made it into paperwork at all: it just hung in the air of the charge-room for a couple of hours until a burst of drunks at closing time gave us something else to think about.

Had they come through to Woodford, they'd have been confronted by Tim Ryan, an inspector well over six feet tall. Great height is useful to policemen, and it is noticeable how many senior officers enjoy its advantages. Not only does it help in fights, but it provides a degree of effortless authority in strained situations. In a freshly creased uniform, Ryan is about as imposing as any policeman can seem. Since a caution is only a stern talking-to, this is just as well.

I met him in civilian clothes. He was comfortable in his chair, and beside Mr Cross seemed a model of hunter's health. But, as we sat in the canteen together, I couldn't take my eyes off our hands: mine folding the ringpull top of a Coke can over and over upon itself until it snapped; Cross's fingers either moving without affecting the rest of his hands, or clenched in something between a prayer and a bout of solitary arm-wrestling; Ryan's long pale fingers looking like boiled sausages twisting just before they split open. At the far end of the room the trainees talked urgently, but it did not seem likely that any of the three of us would ever make cuirassiers.

SIX

The Bloodstained Man

The Bloodstained Man was heavily built, sallow, and pimpled. Cleaned up now, he sat on a comfortable chair with his elbows resting on his thighs and his large, slightly protoplasmic hands clutching each other in Detective Chief Inspector Hilda Harris's office at Barkingside. His voice was slow and tentative. He was really nothing more than an exceptionally gauche adolescent, though twenty years old, who should have been called a boy; but we called him the Bloodstained Man because he thought he'd murdered someone, though he couldn't remember whom or where. We thought he'd probably murdered someone, too, but without a corpse, or a record of anyone missing, interrogating him was difficult.

At first he had appeared to be a victim. Underneath the North Circular Road where it crosses the River Lea is one of those areas of grassy waste which seems quite cut off from the buildings around it: low-rise housing for the most part of this north-eastern end of Wanstead, with about half a mile away, a cluster of council housing, mostly in tower blocks. That was where the bloodstained man had come from one spring afternoon. He had spent the afternoon looking after his younger brother, and sipping the odd can of Special Brew. When his parents came home at four he had gone down to the land by the river with six more cans of Special Brew and a tube of Evo-stik. On closer inspection the grass turns out to be full of litter: one of those eddies at the side of the main current of life where derelicts weighed down by failure quietly sink. He had settled himself comfortably there with the bag and the cans, smeared the glue inside the bag and breathed deeply.

About six o'clock that evening the doorbell of one of the respectable houses nearby rang. When the woman inside opened it, the glue-sniffer collapsed across her threshold. He muttered something about a fight and then passed out, apparently dying. His clothes were drenched in blood from his elbows to his hands and heavily spattered from his stomach to his knees. Even his shoes and face were splashed with blood.

He was taken in an ambulance to hospital at once. But when he arrived and they cleaned the blood away, he was found to be uninjured beneath it. He was not well at all, but that was because of what he had taken. The police could not even start to investigate him until the next morning. When they did so, they became rapidly convinced that he was entirely sincere in failing to remember what had happened the previous afternoon. He could remember sitting down on the grass; and the bag and six cans were later found as he'd described them, but nothing could prompt him to remember what had happened after he had consumed their contents and before he woke up in the hospital.

The investigation soon lost urgency: a report came in that the blood which had been his distinguishing mark was not human. It was thought to have come from an animal, and glue-sniffers have done weirder things than slaughter harmless animals. But no animals were reported missing, any more than humans were. The hospitals were checked: no badly injured men had been received. No lunatics had recently escaped. No bodies had been recovered from the Thames. There was no sign of struggle on the grass where the bloodstained man had been.

The doctor who had reported that the blood was animal

remained puzzled. He had been astonished by its quantity. He thought the most likely source was a cow. This provided another puzzle, for the bloodstained man could not, in his condition, have walked very far to acquire his bloodstains, while the pattern of splashes on his clothes had led the pathologist to suppose that he had been kneeling or crawling in somebody's wounds.

Then a report came back from the laboratory: the bloodstained man had been stained with human blood after all. So now he sat in Hilda's office and worried. He was, I think, more frightened of himself than of the police. He didn't want to be charged with murder, but still less did he want to be a murderer. But most of all he really couldn't remember what he'd done, and he wasn't at all sure that he wanted to remember.

Hilda Harris was gentle with him. What she hadn't seen wasn't worth seeing, her manner suggested, and much of what she had seen wasn't worth seeing either. She has a bantam walk, a light sandpapery voice from smoking and hair the colour of dark sandpaper. She was one of the first women to rise far in the CID, and is still one of the most senior. Since she is a real professional it is impossible to tell how much of her manner is simply a reaction to what is expected of her.

The bloodstained man had not been charged: there was nothing to charge him with. So his interrogation was unencumbered with forms and procedures. I took no notes, concentrating instead on his bewilderment, where he sat two feet from me. This sort of informal conversation suited Hilda:

'I like things to go wallop wallop wallop in interviews and I find it very difficult when pens are scratching away. We had a bloke in the other day and he wouldn't say anything – which takes a lot of doing if you're in a police station – people going at you all the time – you've got to be either a good villain or very very thick.'

The bloodstained man would talk. He had nothing really to express, except a confused trust in his own innocence, for which none of us had any evidence, though we, too, wanted to believe in it. The workings of his glue-crusted brain were slow. He tried to tell Hilda about a girlfriend. But he could not remember her second name, nor where she lived, though he thought she took him home regularly.

Jim Ablett, a CID sergeant, took rough notes of the session. A heavily built man, he had a double-jointed finger, so the stubby pencil he held seemed to stick straight out from his hand. His eyes were set wide apart, and eloquent of disbelief. When the bloodstained man rejected Hilda's idea of a session with a hypnotist, it was he who said that this made things look worse.

Hilda was careful to suggest nothing more than the offer of medical help and reassurance. It would help the bloodstained man himself to be rid of the uncertainty, she said. His large, soft hands moved slowly round each other. I wondered what the advantages of self-knowledge could be for a youth who mixed Special Brew and Evo-stik. After he had gone, to return in a week's time, Jim Ablett was fairly certain of his guilt. Hilda was certain that he was at least being honest. It was agreed to search the housing estate nearest the wasteland in case there were any corpses undiscovered there.

This housing estate was the more respectable of the two on Barkingside's ground. The other, the Eastcheap, was where the serious drug dealers were. It was in the Eastcheap that the corpse of a junkie was found by a caretaker outside one of the lifts. He had died of an overdose of Tuinal and ten pints of beer as well as heroin; when he fell ill he was turned out of the dealer's flat, and the other customers just picked their way over or round him on their way up until the police came.

But the problems of raiding a dealer's flat on the

Eastcheap Estate are immense. The first is that people do not leave carrying the evidence. The flats function as 'shooting galleries': customers go in with money and come out with the heroin concealed in their bloodstream. Once inside, they are protected with double doors, some now reinforced with steel plates so that they cannot be broken down in less than twenty minutes. By that time all the evidence would be drifting down a sewer to the Thames, and the plumbing in these tower blocks is such that twelve floors' worth of sewage emerge in one pipe. Even if one could sift through the evidence it would still be impossible to prove which flat it had come from.

It might seem that steel-reinforced double doors with baulks of wood between them were themselves evidence of some kind of criminal intent. But on an estate infested with junkies everyone needs to take precautions against burglars, and this the dealers could claim to be doing. The same explanations apply to the spyholes, and, in some cases, video equipment that they use to check visitors with.

Given five shooting galleries on one estate, the problem of the Drugs squad becomes apparent. To call it a Drugs squad is perhaps a misnomer: it consists of one man seconded from the Burglary squad, and likely to be returned there if it is decided that burglary is the higher-priority crime. Of course the trade could be driven off the estate. It is all a matter of priorities. If it were a matter of catching suspected police murderers then the resources could be found. Hilda Harris disposes of quite a large CID: in Barkingside alone there are a detective sergeant and four detective constables in the Burglary squad; three male sergeants and seven DCs on the Major Crime squad; a woman detective sergeant and a WDC and two male detectives seconded, when I was there, to a Murder squad.

Any part of the police force that seems well-staffed is

likely to be raided to supply another that is acutely understaffed. J District is the first that is drawn from for 'aid' to places like Wapping. Just as the police in Ilford were using two shifts to cover the twenty-four hours that normally have three at weekends in the spring of 1986 while the third went to Wapping, the Home Beats of the more rural areas were being drawn off on the same mission, and the Drug squad at the local level was quiescent.

This apparent inability to catch known criminals is only surprising if you subscribe to the fallacy of detection. The bloodstained man was the only suspect I came across in four months whose case demanded detective work. Even then, this was not the deduction of the identity of an unknown criminal from a known crime, but of an unknown crime from a suspected criminal – and how that was done will emerge. For the moment it is worth pointing out that practical police work almost always starts from the criminal. First you find out who's done it, and then you find out what he's done. Then you set about proving it, and it is this last which demands the manpower, time and money. The CID in Barkingside were allowed two and a half hours of paid overtime per man per week. Considering that all of them spent at least twenty hours a week doing paperwork or in court, that leaves very little time over.

So if the dealers had to be driven off the estate, this would be at the expense of some other form of police work; and the expense of doing this would be considerable, since to catch and convict a dealer is not simple.

I suppose that with electronic surveillance equipment it would be possible to prove what goes on in the fortified flats of the dealers, most of whom drifted into the business to supply their own habits. According to Jim Ablett, around 80 per cent of the burglaries in the region are drug-related; and while impulsive burglary is easy enough it pays very badly indeed. One man who got away with a haul valued for insurance purposes at £440,000 had sold it for £20,000. Even when allowances are made for a certain inflation of insurance claims, this is still a considerable depreciation; selling heroin is certainly more profitable. According, again, to Jim Ablett, a really heavy heroin habit can costs £200 a day in cash, which represents an awful lot of burglaries. On the other hand one shot of smokable heroin for a beginner costs only a fiver, 'which is a lot cheaper than going down the pub and getting drunk'.

The heroin trade in Barkingside is very well organised. The police believed that there was never more than about a quarter of an ounce of heroin in any dealer's flat at any time. So even assuming that one could bug the flats, or that the curtains were not drawn against the video cameras, a raid which would require weeks of preparation would net little heroin. The ideal then becomes to catch the couriers who bring the stuff round for distribution, and, if possible, the men from whom the couriers get it. But by that time the matter is almost out of the competence of a local Drug squad. There are surprisingly few links in the chain from importer to retailer of drugs. A quarter ounce of cannabis is seldom handled by more than three people between being landed and smoked. Heroin may be handled by rather more people, but that is for reasons of security rather than economics, and as soon as one gets back to the man who employs the couriers who supply the Eastcheap Estate, one is dealing with a criminal important enough to require the attentions of the central Drug squad. And that, of course, is grotesquely overworked, while the Eastcheap is only one estate in what is in policing terms a fairly quiet part of London.

One supplier had been caught in possession of three ounces that year by a detective sergeant. He had been the man who had supplied the Eastcheap, though his place had been taken by the time I arrived. It had taken three weeks of almost continuous surveillance to do it, and the man responsible had then been moved to the regional Crime squad.

Meanwhile, the rumour was even then going around that one of the local 'low-lifes' had started to boast that he kept an unprotected, used hypodermic in his pocket, in the hope that, if he were searched, a policeman would scratch himself and catch AIDS or hepatitis from it. He had confessed to fifty-three burglaries the previous year, but since he was only seventeen was free again. Presumably this is what every junkie will be threatening to do by the time this book comes out. Such fashions spread like milk-drinking among bluetits.

The DS who had caught the supplier had done so more or less in his spare time. He certainly put in a lot more overtime than two and a half hours a week. This sort of thing might embitter policemen when you remember that it was only six months before these happenings that drugs were the most fashionable evil of our times, yet absolutely nothing could be done in practical terms to help catch the dealers. But few seem to be embittered by it. The only outburst of real savagery I heard from a detective came from an armed policeman, who was complaining to his neighbour on a dull journey: 'I fire fifty rounds every four months and get classified on that. A police officer in New York can go down to the firing range and loose off 250 rounds in a day every time he wants to. The public is getting shafted. I joined this force fourteen years ago to serve the public, and we're just not professional enough . . . Bloody amateur fucking training.'

I think that this equability about most crimes arises because there are and will always be so many things for a policeman to do that almost any part of the job can be something done because it is enjoyable. There is an analogy here with journalism, though it is my experience that policemen as a class are a lot fonder of their fellow humans than journalists, among whom are an unhealthy proportion of introverts who write to avoid having to speak to the world. But no journalist complains that there are more interesting (and probably distressing) things happening than he can cover: he worries if there are not.

The analogy really breaks down though when it comes to deciding which crimes are serious. Hilda Harris, who has investigated an awful lot of crime in twenty something years, can seem blasé. One day I came in to her office to talk about the bloodstained man, but she was busy:

'There's a man over at Loughton who is madly in love with his estranged wife, so he hit her over the head four times with a hammer. She's got two skull fractures, a broken jaw, and kidney damage. After he's done it, he goes home and has a cup of tea with his landlady. Then he rings his sister and locks himself in the bathroom. He's obviously doing something to himself, but he's not trying that hard because he unbolts the door when they knock.'

But how else can you tell a story like that, and remain in a condition to act?

The crimes which seem to Hilda most serious are those which involve a betrayal of trust. Murder need not be the most serious crime – an attitude I found later on a murder enquiry, too. This comes out most clearly in her attitude to rape, which is a crime she knows well. While I was there, she was supervising the decoration of a 'rape reception suite', where the victims could be comfortably accommodated while examined and interrogated. It was situated at the back of an old nick, up a flight of stairs, which worried her. Some victims could not, she thought, walk unassisted up the stairs, and there was scarcely room for two people abreast there. But otherwise she was reasonably pleased with the soothing pastel walls, and the shower for ritual as well as physical cleaning as soon as the necessary examinations were over.

Rape is the most spectacular instance of a crime of violation, but there is a sense in which all crimes involve a violation, so that all police work, where it deals with victims of crime, requires that wounds be healed, however technical the job may seem. This applies even to the forensic specialist – Scenes of Crime Officers – of whom the best at Barkingside, by general consent, was Jake, whose second name was also by general consent considered unpronounceable, since he came originally from Nigeria. He started as a fingerprint specialist at Scotland Yard, but after twelve years moved out to become a general purpose SOCO. 'I just thought the job looked interesting, and I've never looked back.'

The SOCOs have a van and a personal radio permanently at their disposal. Their office was larger and barer than most. On one wall hung a poster of Mister T captioned 'No Marks Jake'. The most prominent furniture was a three-foot scaffolding tube, carefully bagged up and labelled. It had been used to smash a phone box. There is hardly any crime which a SOCO does not handle despite the supposition that forensic evidence is reserved for major crimes. As we talked the radio fizzed into blurred speech with a description of a named suspect coming back to the collator's room.

'Half-caste IC3, fuzzy hair, stubby nose, over.'

'He's got previous for burglary, TDA [motor theft]; a right little nurd, over.'

Jake laughed with me. Whatever efforts senior officers might make to conceal the way policemen work, the effort is worthless once you start spending enough time with them. The language will always come through, and it doesn't matter. Still, it's a rare policeman who will trust a writer and one rarer still who will trust a journalist. There is always a suggestion that an outsider must be on the other side. Perhaps that is why Jake was so easy to follow about on a normal day's work.

The previous day there had been nineteen motor vehicle crimes: eight cars stolen, seven broken into, and two vandalised; four reported burglaries: two residential, one school, and a shop; three reported thefts, and two cases of criminal damage. Our first call was to the school, where the video had been stolen over the weekend. It was the ninth school which had been burgled that month, and the robbers had broken in through the skylight, where there were also marks of their predecessors. One school had tried reinforcing the storeroom door with steel, for all the world as if there was heroin inside, but the thieves had simply cut their way through the ceiling.

This school had not bothered. In consequence, the door had been repeatedly jemmied open. New marks overlaid the old ones on the door frame. Jake stood well back at first, peering forwards before he touched anything. Then he mixed up a blue rubbery goo and patted it into place with a palette knife to get a cast of the implement used. He worked with an entranced delicacy, peeling and pulling the blue stuff away with quick, gentle movements, careful not to tear it. Then he dropped it into a labelled plastic bag: these have a fastener which cannot be removed, so that what is inside cannot be taken out without ripping the bag and breaking the tag on it. He brushed fingerprint powder lightly around the door with a limber wrist. There was nothing he expected to find, and nothing was found. If, as seemed likely, the job had been done by pupils, there was no reason why their prints should not be on the door. He explained this to a resigned mistress, and then we set off for the next call.

This was the large mock-Tudor house of a prosperous family. We were served real coffee and decent biscuits in the hall before Jake got to work on the leaded windows by the door. The door itself was substantial, and well-barred, so the thieves had simply pushed through the windows, which offered no resistance. The lead frames had peeled back like an opened banana skin. There was little mess, and only valuables had been stolen from the drawing room; these were professionals. Jake lifted things cautiously, with his fingertips inside them if possible, otherwise touching just the opposite corners. But on their shiny, polished surfaces no marks could be seen. The woman who greeted us was a magistrate, and also well aware that little would come of the work. Jake gathered the glass which had fallen on the carpet, and on the drive outside, but there was nothing to be recovered from the lead frames of the windows.

We returned for lunch: at the next table the young cuirassiers were talking about their anonymity:

'That's what I came into work for: to nick blokes. I know it's the wrong attitude, but that's what I think. There was one bloke I nicked in a red Sierra a month ago, I'd even been in court with him, and had two long interviews. I passed him in a Range Rover, and I thought his face was familiar, so I followed him. Then I stopped him. He'd been interviewed by me twice before and he still didn't recognise me. I said:

"Whose car is that?"
"Me dad's."
"And what's his name?"
"Mr Gibbs."
"And what's your name?"
"Gibbs."
"You're nicked, Humphries!"

'Then he recognized me. I bet his arsehole fell out. I thought he'd bring his heart up: there was this great lump in his throat, hammering. But what's worrying is that the fake name he gave was right. The plates were false, but like any good thief he had got false plates which were right for the model and colour of the car. But these guys were also using the name of the legitimate owner, which is worrying. I wonder if we should check the PNC [Police National Computer] . . . .'

Jake and I left, to visit a house full of music boxes, where a couple of pensioners lived. They were the only people all day to comment on Jake's colour: they were favourably impressed. They served us Nescafé made with boiled milk. Jake did his best to reassure them that whatever had happened would not happen again. They had not been badly burgled. Then he left to spend the afternoon dusting down a car which had been used in an armed robbery. It had been stolen first, so that elimination prints had to be taken from the owners. But he found some good ones on the horn. It is amazing how much people finger the windows of their car doors: as Jake worked, a great spidery mess of greasy marks emerged. I've never known a man to get such wholehearted pleasure from the prospect of getting into a book, perhaps because he has the only police job that cannot be traduced. And to work all one cold afternoon on a car in the open air is a lot more fun than dealing with old corpses, which was the only part of the job he disliked. And Jake has probably been responsible for more convictions than anyone else I talked to. Every court respects forensic evidence.

The other really effective way to catch unidentified criminals is a mass enquiry; and that is the way the mystery of the bloodstained man was cleared up. One windy day twelve men set off to ask everyone in the respectable estate three questions:

> Had they themselves been the victims of a serious assault three weeks ago?
> Did they know anyone who had?
> Did they know anyone living alone who had not been seen for the last three weeks?

The reasons for this were meant to be kept secret, but by the time we reached the third door, everyone knew the story. At ten in the morning, a fair proportion of the women answering their doors are old and deaf. The shouted explanations under echoing concrete must have been audible over half the estate. It was a nice job, full of camaraderie, and chaotic attempts to make sure that every door in the confusingly designed estate was tried. The young men relaxed, and exerted themselves to be friendly. They knew perfectly well that the sight of a policeman unexpectedly on your doorstep suggests bad news. It was a pleasure to them to give good news instead for once. The job was done in a morning, and nothing seemed to turn up, except vague reports of a fight some time ago, but afterwards the sergeant in charge expressed himself delighted:

'We should do more of that. I always say that people judge the whole police force by the first five minutes they come in contact with a policeman, and that was a good way to do it.'

Two days later, Hilda Harris had found what the bloodstained man had done. A Glaswegian from the estate had come into the station to tell the story. On the afternoon the story started, the bloodstained man had finished his beer and glue, as he had said, then gone round for a drink with the Glaswegian. There had been some quarrel – neither of them could remember the details, nor even the cause – and the Glaswegian had smashed a bottle, which cut him on the fleshy part of the hand. He had held it in the air, and the bloodstained man, growing more confused, had somehow – again, the method could not be remembered – managed to smear himself all over with the Glaswegian's blood. Then he had been thrown out. At about the time that the bloodstained man was collapsing over someone else's threshold, the Glaswegian had gone round to the nick to lay a charge of assault, but he was then so drunk that the desk sergeant couldn't understand him, and he went home and forgot the whole thing until the police operation reminded him what had happened.

SEVEN

The Games Room

I did find one murder enquiry in progress while I was doing this book. It is still in progress, as far as I know, so this story, which was told me by one of the men involved, has had various details, such as the identity of the suspects, changed for obvious reasons.

The fire started at about ten to four in the morning, and the brother-in-law woke and smelled smoke about five minutes later. He woke his brother, and found the fire established in the hall and on the stairs. The only way of escape was on to the flat roof at the back. The wife, eight months' pregnant, and her two young sons were sleeping in the front room. They all died, as did the two other children who had been sleeping with the grown-ups. But the two men escaped, with badly burnt hands, after attempting to rescue their children. Even at that time of the morning various people were passing. Two young men tried to help, and two older men actually got a ladder to the front window, but the ladder itself caught fire and drove them back. The louvered windows from the kitchen had been taken out neatly and stacked in the back garden, which is presumably how the arsonist entered the house, though no fingerprints were found there.

The fire brigade were on the scene in a couple of minutes, too late to do more than to establish that an accelerant had been used: in English, that the stairs were drenched with petrol when the fire started, so that no one could have escaped except through the back window. The first four CID officers were there soon afterwards, simply trying to preserve the scene of the crime. As soon as it was known that they were dealing with multiple murder a detective chief superintendent was informed; another ten CID officers came on to the case, and the local Crime squad, eighteen to twenty people, were drafted in. Their job was to do the house-to-house enquiries, which were under-way by half-past five in the morning: the occupants of every house in the road and surroundings were asked who had been there, and whether anyone had seen anything.

By eight in the morning the games room upstairs in the local police station had been cleared out and converted to an incident room. The things needed are kept on hand in every large station.

I was told: 'The system we've developed now is a direct result of the absolute cock-up they made of the Ripper enquiry. The previous system worked well, but it was localised. There was no co-ordination between forces. So it was decided to have a national system. It's designed to be run on a computer, but there are not enough computers to go round; so it is very very labour intensive. By the second day of the enquiry there were eleven office staff here. Under the old system there would have been three.

'All the information comes in to one officer. He assesses it. If it's urgent, then some action is done. If it's routine, it goes to the indexers. There were five girls doing nothing but indexing for thirteen hours a day for the first four months.

'Everything in every statement is cross-indexed. All the names are underlined, and everyone mentioned gets an index card. Every person, vehicle, pub and hospital mentioned got an index card, and they're all cross-referenced on the "action sheets", which record every question asked and every lead checked. There's a special problem with Asian names: you can take statements off three different people, in which three separate names crop up, and they all turn out to refer to the same person.'

On the far wall hung a huge genealogical table of the victims' families, to help clear up that sort of problem. The middle of the room was dominated by a four-tier carousel of these cards: 18,000 of them arranged in circular plastic trays. These conform to a national standard, so that they can rapidly be combined with the results of another enquiry if a similar murder were to happen in the jurisdiction of another force.

Sixty people had worked on the enquiry for the first six months. In all that time the only computing machinery they had was a goldfish in a bowl: on one side was a sticker that said 'yes'; on the other, one that said 'no'. That way, when simple, hard choices had to be made about what to do next, they could ask the goldfish and watch which way it swam. (There was also a budgerigar, which had belonged to a man who had murdered his wife. 'She can't look after it, and he can't have it where he is.')

There were a lot of decisions to be made in the course of the enquiry. From the start, they investigated every aspect of the case they could think of. Separate enquiries dealt with the husband's business; his family; other arson attacks; Fascist groups; local non-political nutters; everyone admitted to hospital with burns in the following days, since the fire must have started with such a whoosh as to burn the hands of whoever laid it; the leisure and social lives of the victims; and an allegation of a previous arson attempt at the address.

This last line of enquiry was quickly dismissed as a red herring: 'Everything they got wrong in the first "incident" was right in the second one. But none of the family told us about this. They've done nothing but lie to us from the start. But simple humanity says they've gone through enough. We've investigated forty separate crimes in the course of this one murder enquiry. We can't offer immunity, but if we could, we would. But there is no evidence whatsoever that this was a racial attack.

'One of the WPCs in the area has got a degree in statistics, so she was told to make a statistical analysis of all the cases of arson on the ground over the last few years. She discovered that if you were an Asian you had a 2.5 per cent greater chance of being the victim of arson than if you were white. But nobody listens to that sort of thing. The press is just determined that it's all racial. There was a big piece in the *Observer,* where they listed eleven arson attacks on Asians. They didn't mention that eight of those have been cleared up, and not one was racial.

'But we've had a lot of negative return from the press. Basically we've been trying to reconstruct the scene, and we came up with a red Cavalier and a red Celica that we couldn't identify. So we used *Police 5* and *Crimewatch*: we've done video reconstructions of people climbing. Nothing helped.

'We've investigated all similar arson attacks: for instance, there was one in Hastings on a white family about a fortnight later where petrol had been splashed up the stairs at 4 a.m.; and there was one in Grimsby, but these weren't the same. They only used a couple of pints of petrol.

'We've got a computer readout on every red Toyota Celica in the country, and of every red Cavalier. We interviewed the owners of every single one.'

Nothing came of that, either. Nor did other murderers stop for the convenience of this enquiry. After five months the enquiry team was reduced to forty men after a youth had been buggered and murdered in the north of the ground. They started that enquiry by investigating all known sex criminals, and as a side-effect found one in the special wing of Rochester prison who had been writing to

his male lover about what they would do together once he
was free again. They were planning to break into a
maternity home and bugger and disembowel a newborn
baby.

After six months of the arson enquiry, they reckoned
that they had, by elimination, decided who had done it.
Officers were sent to Canada and to Pakistan in search of
evidence, but after a further four months the detectives
had come to believe that they would never be able to
prove their suspicions. When I was in the games room
there were only fifteen men left working on it, and no end
in sight. The man I was talking to was alone in the games
room at 11 a.m. After a while we moved to the pub to
talk, leaving the goldfish to its own devices.

'I've been doing nothing but murders since 1979,' he
told me. 'I finished training on a new system we'd just
brought in then, on 22 December, and I was called out
for the first time on 25 December. This isn't a good job for
family life.

'The training's very good, but they're very bad at using
it. Like when I joined the CID, I got a ten-week intensive
course in criminal law, and it was excellent. Then they
dump you in an office and leave you to rot until you've
forgotten it all. And the law's changed a lot since then,
but we're never retrained to bring us up to date. The
whole basis of our job changed with the Criminal Justice
Bill. PACE is another example. It's given us all sorts of
niggling powers: just enough to annoy the public. We can
arrest someone for littering now, stuff like that; and it's
taken away almost all the powers we need to catch
criminals. And no one's been told about it, or trained
properly.

'Most murders are solved in the first couple of days. If
it's not solved in a week you know you've got a sticker.
It's one of those crimes where you have to get yourself on
the same wavelength as the people involved, whatever

126

that is. If it's something in a rich suburb, then you've got to talk with the people in a different way. It's not normally a difficult crime to solve. You've got to have a motive and an opportunity, but that's not usually too difficult to find. Planning and deliberation are rare when it's a motiveless crime: when it's happened almost as an incident.

'There's very little scope for murders really. Mostly they're domestic or GBH gone wrong, when they set out to beat somebody up and go a little too far. But it's got much more common since they abolished capital punishment. I know that's not what the figures say, but if you count manslaughter in as well, then it's gone sky high: by about 300 per cent, and the law changed in 1982 to make manslaughter a more probable verdict than murder.

'No, I don't reckon murder is the worst crime of all, at least it needn't be. Rape, incest, some buggeries can all be worse. But of course it's treated differently from all other crimes. If we put these resources into anything else, we could clear that up, too. What's really frustrating is when you get someone admitting to it – and still he's acquitted. I mean, he takes it all back in the box, and claims he was pressured into confessing. It's usually much easier to get a confession for a murder than for a burglary. I suppose people want to get it off their chests.'

I never met a detective who believed that people confessed to things they hadn't done. I think this belief in confessions is justified so long as one distinguishes between major and minor crimes. Much later I was talking to some colleagues of the Home Beat officer who had clouted a man on the ground at Wapping. The HBOs hated Wapping duty, and when they discussed it, it was from a purely functional point of view. One had a story of a man who'd been nicked for kicking a police horse on the night when his colleagues had sticked a demonstrator: 'Now they fitted him up with a load of other stuff –

127

resisting arrest, threatening behaviour, assault – and the funny thing was that he put his hands up to all that. But he wouldn't have the horse. Probably sensible of him. In this country it's much more serious being cruel to animals than belting a police officer.'

But the rules for a 'hurly-burly' are different from those which govern normal crimes, and that sort of misdemeanour will not bring you into the hands of the CID. Its members do not believe they charge innocent people. Hilda Harris, like others, says that people simply don't confess to things they haven't done. I knew a man who boasted that in three years he never charged anyone who wasn't convicted. He certainly never charged anyone he didn't believe was guilty.

The man from the games room never quite told me who he thought was guilty. He was trying not to tell me at all, and for parts of our conversation I laid my notebook down. But the murders had preyed on his mind almost as much as they must have consumed the murderers'. I began to see why people confess. It is not so much to be free of guilt as to share an overwhelming knowledge in the hope that one can thus make sense of it. In this sense, the detective needs to share his knowledge of the crime quite as much as the criminal, perhaps more if his moral sense is more delicate. If it is necessary to understand the criminal to find him, then a murder squad detective must also be able to share the horrible knowledge of the fact of murder. His voice, when he described which bodies had been found where and in what attitudes, was full of pain and anger nearly a year after the events. He must have lived with this detailed knowledge all that time.

So it was impossible for him to talk with me for two or three hours about his job without showing what he thought. He was much of a professional to be able to hide what he thought important, just as he was too much of a professional to tell me. And, no, he saw as few police officers as possible in his spare time. He'd garden or do anything rather than talk shop, because most of it was, after all, extremely boring if you weren't doing it.

Back at Ilford, Chief Superintendent Robinson greeted me with pleasure. He had just been sent a form reporting a racial incident, as the new system demands. Every racial incident – one in which the participants are of different ethnic groups – must be reported to a chief superintendent, and records must be kept of what is done to follow it up. This is, I think, a largely cosmetic system. It is worth the trouble, but it will catch few criminals: it is part of the symbolic and not the pragmatic role of the police. Mr Robinson read to me with relish from the sheet of paper:

'Mr White stated, "these Pakistanis can't drive round all cocky." Mr White is black. That's a racial incident, isn't it, Anj?'

EIGHT

Pastoral

The National Front does exist in J District. I found it in
Loughton, the most northerly police station in the Met.
Out there one has left London altogether, and is in Essex,
on the edge of Epping Forest. The country towards
London is mostly rolling fields, or seems so, when you
trundle through the lanes in a panda. Passing one gentle
rise of extremely expensive houses with views out over the
countryside, the driver remarked: 'Everyone who lives in
this road is a villain. Some of them's bent villains, and
some of them's straight. But they're all villains.'

There is very little detected crime in this prosperous
belt, and I had expected there would be even less in
Loughton. Of course I was quite wrong. Since Loughton
is in essence a small town rather than a part of London,
there is a great deal of nastiness going on under the
surface. The collator's cards, which hang on the walls,
listing local criminals, seem to have been written by a man
who enjoys this. The comments on character are more
frequent and nastier than most places: 'Violent, Suicidal,
Sniffs glue', or just 'Well at it'.

The nick is Victorian and pleasantly scruffy. It seems a
long way from the newer buildings closer to London;
prisoners who are taken to Barkingside to be charged
make a trip of eight miles, which seems a long way to all
involved. There are cells at the back of Loughton nick,
but they are only used to take the overspill from prisons.
When I was there the prison officers were working to rule,

and three unfortunates were cooped up in the old tiled cells. It was hot enough to make one feel thirsty, yet simultaneously somehow damp.

The sergeant back there was sympathetic, which struck me as odd. Since the prisoners had all been charged and refused bail, they were all presumably guilty, in police terms, of rather nasty crimes. Yet there seemed to be none of the normal feeling that criminals get what they deserve when they suffer. Perhaps this was because the men in the cells were completely powerless. Policemen are frequently kind, and, in so far as one can generalise, they are very keen on doing things for charity: they will run marathons, raffle things, and put enormous amounts of energy into the sort of worthy causes which do good things in bad taste, like the Rotary Club. But it is only exceptional ones who seem to regard the criminals they deal with as objects of sympathy. Their prime job is to stop criminals, not to understand them.

Sympathy for the law abiding is a different matter: it is part of professionalism, though not the most attractive part to the young cuirassiers. One of the HBOs there is a woman with thirteen years' service, Mandy Bennett: on the day of the local elections she was sent out to soothe a National Front candidate who had received death threats. They were in the form of graffiti on his election literature, which had been shoved through his letterbox the previous night. That was what frightened him, because he was standing as a candidate in Hackney, a long way away. How had his address become known?

He was in his thirties, unemployed, and growing a little fat, with chipmunk jowls behind a small sloping chin. He handled the paper carefully by the edges, and knew the routine involved. He had in fact himself been a policeman for a few months, years ago. He brought this fact out as part of the credentials of his case, so to speak: the roughly written message, 'You're dead,' seemed as grotesque as the leaflet it defaced. He claimed to be really worried that these things would frighten his children. His council flat was cluttered with family mess, but sparsely furnished: the kitchen floor was plain linoleum; a large white bicycle leant against a dirty white wall. A child's drawing of 'Daddy' was pinned to the wall above it. A television played in the room beyond, and I caught a glimpse of a child in the garden beyond that.

As we left, I remarked cruelly that this had been a job which would have been better done by a black PC. Mandy Bennett was gently apologetic about the candidate. A lot of the wrong people joined the Force, she said, but they soon learnt their mistake. But she did not approve of his standing as a candidate in Hackney. If he held those beliefs, he ought to have defined them where he lived, she thought – though she could see that it might have been more frightening to live in Hackney and be an NF candidate.

It was pleasant to perform the symbolic functions of the police with this steady plain woman on the sort of bright spring day when any sensible person is fishing. We travelled round the polling stations set up in schools and church halls. It was difficult to find any voters, let alone any engaged in sharp practices. The ballot boxes themselves were the only bits of machinery I have ever seen that were older than police typewriters; and their various custodians were almost as old. Mandy chatted with everyone. Partly she was checking that nothing untoward had happened; partly proving that everything was all right by her presence. Talking is almost the whole of her job when she's not puttering around in a Mini Metro. The only contact with the job was her personal radio, which was tuned in to the station frequency, so that there was not even the sputter of the Met radio, which deals with 999 calls, to remind us of the dramas beyond. We drove through hilly roads lined with brightly painted Chelsea-ish houses that debouched almost without warning into the forest, and talked about riding through the glades. Out here she was a more effective officer for being seen. In London it's almost always more effective to be invisible.

Back at the station there were two CID officers from Leman Street, who thought that an escaped prisoner might be heading out this way. Heavy and dark, with practised beetling stares, they moved around the office or peered through the windows, swearing frequently, but he didn't turn up.

We drove off again, to see if anyone had parked where he or she shouldn't. Mandy had a special form for such occasions: not a parking ticket, but a piece of paper which said that just this once she was going to be nice and let them off. She walked down the shopping street, looking into every shop to enquire about thieves or whatever, making herself known. Compared to the boredom and discomfort of policing a football match from a place where you can't see the game, this seemed an easy part of the job. Yet it was not nearly as much fun, nor as satisfying, since her presence did not seem to be accomplishing anything. Even the gentlest parts of police work derive their interest from the fact that they change the way the world is and affect people. Showing a reassuring presence to shopkeepers who do not feel threatened seemed to me about as much fun as changing the ribbon on a typewriter; but to Mandy, who likes human contact, this was an important part of the job. Late at night in Area Cars I had seen a fair number of fish-and-chip shop owners and so on, but they were gratified by our visits, and sold discounted snacks to prove it.

The next day seemed less eventful, but it was a great deal more satisfying: it was Mandy's day for touring old people's homes. Her special care there was for police widows. It's really only fair that policing, a vocation which has broken up so many marriages, should provide a family for the old. The twin stresses of work and solitude are unlikely to promote longevity; but Mandy was meticulous in her attentions to the police widows on her beat.

We visited three homes in one morning, and were fêted with milky coffee and biscuits everywhere we went. Mandy spoke to every inmate she found, continuing, in most cases, conversations that had gone on for months as she visited them; admiring photographs of grandchildren and great-grand-children, remembering names, listening carefully, and saying undemanding things clearly to keep the talk going. The radio drew us away from the last home with a tale of stray cows on one of the roads.

There is not even a police canteen at Loughton, which greatly civilises the nick. Food is collected from a bakery down the road. While Mandy did her paperwork I settled with a sandwich and a cup of tea in the collator's room, where a copy of the Meynell Report had been pinned on the wall. This was the account by the policewoman who ran the Home Beats on Broadwater Farm estate of all that she thought had gone wrong in the run-up to the riots. It made a splash when the *Daily Mail* had published it, but to get the full flavour it should be read in a police station, occasionally interrupted by officers saying that it was all that was worth reading about the Force.

The 'report' was written the morning after the riot; and Couch disputes most of what it says. Nor did an enquiry find anything to act on. But, if not a picture of fact, it is at any rate a portrait of a mood. It shows where the Met would be without hope. Couch had tried to police the Broadwater Farm estate as if the inhabitants could be brought to see, if the police behaved reasonably and tolerantly, that the Force was in fact reasonable and tolerant. This was not a tremendous break with tradition. Hilda Harris had served on the estate some years before, and told me that large, lounging blacks would blow dope smoke in her face as she passed, and see whether she was frightened as a result. She reckoned that you were all right as long as you showed no fear. Things got worse by the time WPS Meynell took up the job; even the maps of the estate at the station were outdated, she said.

I had been on the Farm the day and night after the riots, when you could hardly look anywhere without seeing a clump of policemen. Even then it was easy to get lost in the grey windy concrete walkways and find yourself surrounded by tatty wooden doors in dirty stairwells. The lifts, of course, were broken. Even for a visitor there seemed to be no way out. A couple of WPS Meynell's Home Beats had been surrounded in such a place. They were told – and believed – that if they radioed for help they would be killed. Then the Asian HBD 624 Babu was told that he would be killed anyway as a traitor to his race if he continued to patrol the estate. When the pair returned to base, very badly shaken, Meynell tried to get Babu transferred. He was terrified, she said. Couch wouldn't let him go. He was to show great bravery himself when the riot came, and it was not bad leadership to demand of his men nothing that he wouldn't do himself. Besides, policing in extreme situations depends on courage. But there is a distinction between leadership and management, and it is bad management to lead where others cannot follow.

The force and anguish of Meynell's report came from its theme: that senior officers simply did not understand what her men were facing. She told Couch that a riot was imminent: he ignored her. She brought him drug bags. He threw them away. Even petrol bombs disappeared in the station, she said, unless they had been logged by a soco. Tangmere and Stapleford, the central blocks of the estate, outside which PC Blakelock would be murdered, became no-go areas for the police that summer. The Home Beats dared not patrol them in twos: a group of policemen large enough to be safe would have seemed a provocation, and could hardly have arrested anyone. The evidence would have gone by the time they closed in. So drugs were dealt in openly beneath the tower blocks.

This Meynell regarded as outrageous racial prejudice on Couch's part. She drew a bitter comparison with the 'Peace Convoy' – another anti-police group which contained a hard core of serious, violent drug dealers – and the Stonehenge Festival, which had been broken up with whatever force was necessary and a bit more besides. 'But that festival was for the benefit of white drug dealers.'

No one believed Meynell, she wrote, when she said the estate would blow up. And when it did, no use was made of the contingency plan to storm the estate. Instead the riot was simply contained for the first six hours. This was partly because most of the information except Meynell's suggested that Wood Green, where there are shops to loot, would be the scene of any trouble; and, had the fighting spilled out of the estate it would have caused much more damage. But Meynell knew, and PC Babu knew, that the purpose of any riot would not be to enrich the rioters, but to give the police 'a bloody good hiding'.

This is all a long way from Loughton, where my reflections were interrupted by a bomb scare. A suspect package had been found in a bus station, and a couple of PCs were despatched to deal with it. 'Piss off, then,' said the inspector, and a voice from outside added: 'If I may put it that way, without respect, sir.' They pissed off, without respect. The MP radio started to talk about a white male, 'fifteen to sixteen years old', carrying a sawn-off shotgun, who was escaping from a robbed petrol station in Hackney. The men who had been to the bus station returned: they had found only a harmless parcel.

Mandy Bennett's next call came through on the ordinary telephone: not the 999 system, nor even the personal radio. Somebody's ex-husband was 'making misery' in the house of her new family; and we drove off without undue haste through what had become a peaceful evening. The road was a stub-end of brick council houses, facing a field that was just turning a dark, blurred green at its far edge. She parked some little way away, so as not to make what was happening too obvious to the neighbours.

As we moved down the road a rufous man with vehement blue eyes walked up, apparently glad to see us. He was of middle height and slim build. He spoke without gestures or noticeable exaggeration, but was none the less eager to get his retaliation in first, which he did by explaining that the others in the house would slander him when they had the chance. He claimed that his ex-wife and her new husband had pushed him from the house after refusing him right of access to his daughter: 'She had an affair and broke up two families,' he said, as if this clearly justified him in whatever he might do for the rest of his life. He had himself remarried. He talked to me, not Mandy, when he could. As usual in situations where normal clothes were interpreted as plain-clothes, I kept as quiet as I could. I certainly wasn't about to introduce myself unless I had to; and if people are expecting you to be wise, sympathetic, and non-committal it is surprisingly easy to act that way. As a general rule, only the guilty ever noticed that I was not a policeman.

The vehement man didn't want anything dramatic done: he was careful to qualify the shove as no more than 'common assault', about which the police can do nothing. This was the sort of thing that always made me sympathise with those policemen who claim that the Force is handicapped now that people know their rights. It sounds – and sounded, the first time I heard it – a frightful thing to say. Yet one night in Ilford, a raucous cat-like noise on a wet street drew the panda car to a couple of teenagers fighting. She was drunk and bedraggled, teetering on her shoes; he seemed to be half pulling her, half holding her upright. One had the impression that he had been hitting her recently. He, too, looked as if he had spent some time in one of the hedges guarding the quiet, small houses around.

'Just a domestic disturbance, officer,' they said, and the officers had to agree. I don't know whether that couple should have known their rights, but it seemed, and still seems an affront that they should know the jargon which would allow him to get away with hitting her. It's a trivial case, but 95% per cent of all police work is trivial. Certainly the work that makes them popular seems trivial in the statistics.

The scarlet woman who had had the affair and broken up two families turned out to be fat and mouse-kindly, with a quiet, dignified husband. The little girl at the heart of it was out of the room while the story went on. There was a long, tangled history of unpaid alimony and the arbitrary exercise of visiting rights. They did not deny pushing him from the house: they claimed that this was the only way to avert a scene. What really concerned them was that the little girl did not want to do whatever her father had planned for her the next day. Careful questioning from Mandy elicited the fact that this was true: she had some treat planned which she did not want to give up at short notice.

So Mandy went and told the vehement man, where he waited outside, a little down the road, that he had no chance. He seemed to lose his enthusiasm for a civil action. It might have been a nothing visit, requiring no more than intelligence, experience, tact, and sympathy to conclude successfully. Not, perhaps, a job for the cuirassiers, though they would certainly end up doing jobs like that; but, brooding on the way it might have been handled, or might have turned out had the participants not agreed in advance that disputes are not settled, only postponed, by the use of force, I wondered to what extent the police are agents as well as beneficiaries of civilised standards. It's easy to see that a brutish HBO could have made the matter worse. Does a good one make it better?

That is the essential problem if the 'inner cities' are to be brought back under control. The prime need for the police is to keep them under physical control: 'to rule the streets'. This on its own leads to something like the military doctrine of 'minimum force', which, incidentally, requires far more manpower than does maximum force: one pilot in a fighter bomber could have subdued, or at least flattened, Broadwater Farm all on his own. I'm not saying he should have done; the point of the example is to show that policing cannot be reduced to a matter of force, even if it is inconceivable without the use of force.

This is not quite the same as saying that the police cannot do it all on their own. The 'multi-agency' approach promoted by Sir Kenneth Newman, and used, for example, by the Child-Care squad involves co-operating with the social services and the local political structures; yet carried to its logical conclusion it would still confine the importance of the police to their judicious use of force. They might become something like the cutting edge of society, instead of seeming cut off from it, but they would still only be the cutting edge. That is not enough.

One night in an Area Car in Ilford we got a call to a 'disturbance' on the fringes of Dagenham. It turned out to be a black woman with huge eyes and her paler, even huger-eyed child who were being comforted by a white neighbour with a great wattle on her throat. The frightened woman's uncle had threatened her with a knife and then run out into the surrounding estate. He was living with her because the only alternative was to return to a mental hospital, but drink did not agree with him. She had been terrified even to go out to the phone box which served the area. As they now prepared to leave the house, reassured by Rachel's presence, it occurred to me that the atmosphere of the blitz must have been a lot like this. The woman who was comforting them was probably bombed herself, and resettled after the war; it was that type of estate.

The living room had a fragile look. It was sparsely furnished, and there were frail pretty fabrics piled in a corner. The neighbour made tea, and talked eagerly while Rachel was upstairs helping the frightened woman dress. Even to stub a cigarette out in a saucer felt like a burglar's desecration, but at last it was over, and the woman and her daughter set off towards relatives in Hackney. Rachel radioed in her report; and as we drove away said to the saturnine Peter, 'Well, that's it then. She was sleeping with the uncle, but the child's not his. Why? Oh, it kept him out of the hospital. I got the whole story out of her while she was dressing.'

It will always be the police who come in to situations like that before almost anyone does. Force is of no use; and little else is of any use. But if the police cannot act in small and unpretentious ways as a civilising influence even in unpropitious surroundings, their cuirassiers will always be outnumbered. This may not matter too much on the fringes of Dagenham, or in Loughton, where the misery is confined to small pockets. At Leyton, where J Division touches the 'inner city', it matters a great deal.

NINE

Out of Order

'Lost black dog if fund
He live at 85 Bulwer Road Leytonstone
He's name is blacky.'

That, pinned on the noticeboard in front of the station
counter at Leyton, shows at once the distance from
Loughton, and the further distance from the geographi-
cally closer Woodford Green. Leyton is not a front-line
station. It's just that people round there can't read or
write. The young PCs are warned not to turn their backs
on anyone who might have a knife, but there is only one
estate on the ground marked down as the possible scene
of a riot. The streets around are full of the sights of
modern poverty: secondhand furniture shops which
advertise their willingness to do DHSS estimates; small
private fast-food shops because the big chains do not find
the trade worth their while; newsagents where all the
magazines are printed on thin paper and the cheapest
cigarettes are most prominently displayed. The clothes shops
display shiny trousers and thin bomber jackets in their
windows. Even peacocks' feathers would be warmer.

Down in the canteen where the young cuirassiers
lounge with their clip-on ties discarded, the informality of
their manner and posture makes their shirts seem whiter
and stiffer. Only a young inspector – twenty-five-years
old, graduate entry, two years on the streets, and then a
special course at Bramshill – never seemed to relax. For

Leyton is a place where the new styles of policing have
formed new administrative methods. This the sort of
place where Kenneth Newman's ideas, and management
jargon, have struck root; whereas Ilford, though just as
rough a ground, was run on a much more personal,
unsystematised basis while I was there.

The collator's room at Ilford came to seem a sanctuary
for me. Once the station had an open day, and the table in
the snooker room was covered to display the snakes
collected by one of the PCs who had worked in a zoo
before he took up policing. His pride was a great warm
python which weighed down my shoulders when he
wrapped it on my neck so that the visiting schoolgirls
squeaked and reached out delicate hands to touch it.
Stories were told about his inviting grown-up women back
to the flat who had panicked when they discovered an
unexpected snake on the sofa. Some of them might even
have been true. Upstairs a team from the forensic
laboratory south of the river had a display in somebody's
office, and would show the grown-ups pictures of a
barbecue in which an erring husband had disposed of his
inconvenient wife:

'Nothing left but some grease in the cracks on the
patio.'

Mr Robinson was being hearty in his office to one of the
local MPs and his wife; but if some secrets were revealed,
others were hidden for the day. Even the door to the
collator's room was concealed behind a couple of bright
posters about crime prevention, so I locked my jacket and
notebook in there. I had been warned that anything not
nailed down on open days was likely to be stolen by a
curious visitor. By seven in the evening, things were
beginning to return to normal. Almost all the visitors had
gone, and with them the people who had been working in
the collator's room. No one left had a key.

'No problem!' they said in the radio room. 'There's a

milk-crate in the yard. That's what we keep it for. Just climb in through the window.' So I did. I was just wriggling out under the window with my legs hanging over the courtyard and my jacket on the sill when Mr Robinson and a deputy assistant commissioner left the nick by the back door and emerged about a yard away, with their eyes on a level with my feet. Their eyelids did not even flicker at the sight of a scruffily dressed man heaving himself out of the window of the most secret room in the station. Apart from introducing me to the DAC as a man who worked for the *New Statesman,* Mr Robinson made no attempt to take advantage of the situation.

The collator's room at Ilford was used a lot, but no one could call it the hub of the station. At Leyton things were different: the collator there was not an old, experienced man, but Andy, a young graduate who would rather have been on the streets, not that he had any choice in the matter.

'The thing that shocked me when I started this job,' he said, 'was the sheer number of criminals there are. There's a game we play on trains called "Spot the CRO". In any carriage coming into work you'll see some.' CRO is short for Criminal Records Office, and hence for the numbered records kept there. A third of all adults under twenty-eight have convictions, according to the Home Office; and while there will always be enough crimes to employ any number of policemen, the problem for the Met is that there are too many criminals – a rather different figure, which more policemen might do some-thing about, if there were room in the jails for them, which there is not.

At Leyton, the approach taken is analogous with the military surgeon's practice of triage – the division of incoming casualties into three groups: those who will probably die whatever the surgeon does; those who will probably survive whatever he does; and those for whom his attentions will make a real difference, The analogy is not exact, for the more serious the injury, the less likely the surgeon is even to attempt to repair it, whereas really serious crimes get the undivided attention of the police. But in both systems trivial cases are likely to be ignored, and both depend on intelligent selection of incoming problems.

That is why a graduate PC sits in the collator's room at Leyton with a woman sergeant, and every Tuesday morning briefs the Priority Policing Group, a mixed squad of CID and uniformed branch who mostly operate in plain-clothes. It is in the nature of policing that a PC will often tell senior officers what they have to do: he has the information. But the way it happens in Leyton is unusual.

I was sitting in the collator's room one Monday afternoon with Andy and Cathy, the sergeant, arguing about whether the police were sexist and racist. Cathy maintained they were. I argued against this proposition in general, and Andy just hated the idea of 'the police' being anything as a group. 'An uncle came up to me at a family party, and asked me, "What sort of music do policemen listen to?" Policemen! So I told him "The Ride of the Valkyries", and that seemed to keep him happy.'

We were still enjoying this when a man like an oak tree walked in. He was about six and a half feet or perhaps two metres tall, with a dark dished face so forceful it took some time to realise that it was not also ugly, and huge eyebrows. Thick hair covered his arms and sprouted above the neck of his T-shirt like tangled twigs. He was waiting for a solicitor to see his prisoner.

'Thieving Scotch git. Nicked him down the DHSS. Pockets full of money. He had 200 quid in his pockets, but even burglars got to have their dole. I'd like to see how he explains the 200 quid away.'

He walked around the room as he spoke, addressing his remarks to all of us.

'And now there's a bloody queue of solicitors at £50 an hour for people like him. If I had my way we'd nick them all for conspiracy. They're all guilty of conspiracy. And they rip these poor bastards off.'

And he was gone. 'That's just Matt. He hates everybody. He's not racist; he's not sexist. He just hates everybody,' said Cathy. The next day I discovered that he was the head of the PPG: a former journalist named Matt Johnson, whom I grew to like and esteem as much as anyone on the job. The extravagance and vigour of his language would have been attractive in any case. So many of the cuirassiers stole what they know of police language from Joseph Wambaugh (and Wambaugh's later novels stole it from his early ones) that the ones who spoke an English demotic always came as a surprise.

I'm still not certain whether the police have a dialect of their own. There is certainly a policeman's style of narration off-duty; then there is the language they have to use in court, which sounds like the autobiography of a tape recorder. Scotland Yard has its own excruciating jargon, in which problems are 'impacted' by 'proactive' officers. There are police stories:

Last night at about twenty to seven there was an incident involving three black youths in a Fiat and two whites in a Transit. The Fiat cuts the Transit up; and everyone stops for an altercation. The blacks claim the whites had been shouting racial abuse at them. Anyway, after a while one of the blacks reaches into the boot of the car; gets out a jack; and throws it through the windscreen of the Transit.
Which would have been all right except that it collected a passenger's head and he's got about seven skull fractures and is probably going to die.

But plenty of people tell stories that well, even if few

145

journalists can. And police jargon is curiously limited. There are only about fifty words or abbreviations used in the Met which are not immediately intelligible. You could not tell a policeman off-duty by listening to his language. But there remains a recognisable police style, which I think came across from their concern with truth: with what actually happens, rather than what we wish might happen, or clumsily believe the world is like because it ought to be. This is not to say that they don't have ludicrous prejudices, like everyone; and that quite a lot of these prejudices are held by many policemen and by few outside the Force. But I could not now identify a single police prejudice, though I could probably have produced a dozen before I started watching policemen work. The more I met, the more it became obvious that they were all individuals, until at last I was as puzzled, though not as offended, as Andy in the collator's room when asked what 'policemen' in general liked, or thought. The highest ambition of this book is to suggest how they think.

Their work depends on accurate observation of the way things really are and the ways in which real people behave. These things are frequently not so much shocking as incredible. The only reason why we are not properly shocked is that we don't believe what we see. That happens to bad policemen too. On this argument, the objection to racism and sexism is that they entail believing things that are not true; and hence stop us being as shocked by the real world as we ought to be. Some policemen are like that; this makes them not only unpleasant, but unprofessional, since it means that they cannot do properly that part of their job which does not rely on other people's expectations of their uniform.

'Professional' is a word I came to dislike when used by the police, since it usually threatened an incomprehensible burst of management jargon. But the substance was enjoyable.

Eight people attended the weekly PPG briefing: four from the CID. They clustered round the DIIU (District Intelligence and Information Unit) table while Andy read out the week's crimes. The point of the system is to identify the places where effort is worthwhile: the people to nick; the places to watch them. It was extremely informal, as the meetings of professionals going about their business are. A Xeroxed collator's card was passed around:

'Stick a bloke on him from 6–2. He's just come out from doing a porridge. Out on parole. And since he came out we've had all these shopbreakings; entry from the rear. He probably works with his brother, but they live on Walthamstow section. Get a couple of your better officers to watch him, Matt.'

'Now this one's a good, professional breaker.'

The detective inspector who took charge of the meeting, Robin Jackson, was a little Ulsterman so dapper he made me feel I had been up all night in a gutter, stealing from tramps. He seemed to bounce as he reported from an earlier meeting:

'I also said we'd look at this music place. Possible handling [of stolen goods]. It's just a feeling.'

Another card was passed round:

'Very interesting shop. Even worse.'

'That's a firearms place, that is.'

'Well, we should get a flavour of it just from looking for a couple of hours; but carefully.'

Matt Johnson announced that he had a couple of men watching a pusher that afternoon, from three till seven: surveillance may sound glamorous, but from an administrative point of view it is still time spent doing other things, which will have to be done later, on overtime.

The triage was not done at the briefings in the collator's room. Occasionally the maps and collations of an area would throw up a pattern of crimes which suggested a promising line of enquiry, but most of the work of that sort was done by two officers on the Crime Desk. They had replaced the Beat Crime and the Burglary squads, and their most frequent job was to decide to do nothing about a crime, and do it well. This makes a lot of sense. The previous year, there had been 4,500 autocrimes on this station's ground: 7,000 beat crimes in all. The Beat Crime squad had varied in size between four and five officers, and they had had to do their own paperwork too.

When crime is that common it overwhelms even usually effective routines: to dust down a car properly for fingerprints takes about two hours for a SOCO (who is paid no overtime). There are only 8,760 hours in a year. So ordinary stolen cars don't get checked. This still leaves a lot of crime to deal with. In the first half of 1986, up to 24 June, when I talked to the sergeant at the Crime Desk, he had that year recorded 1,405 'minor crimes' – which are not, as he pointed out, minor to their victims; 1,355 burglaries, and 1,450 major crimes: robbery, deception, crimes of violence; oh, and 2,264 autocrimes.

What the Crime Desk does about all this is to write personalised letters, from one of the computer systems which the police really seemed to appreciate on J Division. Most people who report crimes get these; and a phone call. The purpose of this is to show that the police sympathise without raising pointless hopes that anything more effective will be done than taking elimination prints from the people who ought to have left fingermarks all over their homes. What the Desk can, and does, accomplish more than that is to put people in touch with the victim support schemes; these are phoned every day to keep a functioning liaison going.

One would have thought that this withdrawal from vast areas of crime would have depressed the policemen involved. Instead it seemed to have exhilarated them. Part of this was simply relief at not having to pretend any more that they could do everything the public expected of them. Chief inspectors are not stupid men; Dave Solman, who told me about the system, seemed to derive pleasure beyond the simple lack of pretence from the thought that he could now put intelligence into the job.

'We're actually realistic enough now to know what we can and can't do; and I think it's giving a better service to the public than the old system where a man goes round and nothing happens.'

The system at Leyton is very well worked out and formalised, with its regular briefings and liaisons. For that reason alone it is likely to spread, since an irregular, personalised style of organisation like that at Ilford, while it may work as well, cannot be taught; it depends too much on the personality of the man at the top. But police work is by its nature irregular and particular, like history; and theories of policing, like schemes of history, are only valuable as instruments, not in themselves. No matter how elegant and lucid the schemes at the top may seem, things are always a mess at the bottom level.

But they can be an exhilarating mess. Late one afternoon I went out in an unmarked car with some of the PPG. 'Right, lads,' said one of them, 'We're going out on the streets to combat fucking PACE and catch the bastards bang to rights.' We never did. Jeff, the driver, terrified me. He did not drive worse than Area Car men; nor did he drive quite so fast. But other drivers, pedestrians, and so on, expect that sort of driving from a large, clearly marked police car, not from a little nondescript saloon. Jeff did everything at full tilt, and was greatly esteemed by his superiors as a result. Small and vehement, with thinning red hair, he seemed at first the embodiment of a nasty policeman, largely because he was quite uninhibited in conversation. 'If you can't take a joke,' he'd say, changing an old army saying, 'you shouldn't have been born.'

One afternoon in the canteen he kept repeating a newly acquired statistic: 'D'you know, there's 147 different bacteria in a woman's minge. Think of that,' he said to a WPC; then added, after she had gone, unimpressed, 'Still, I don't mind a bit of muff-diving myself, so long as it's clean.' His memories of Hendon were, for public consumption, exclusively sexual. He was pursued through the Force by a story of how he had taken a woman cadet out to the playing fields one night. They were getting along wonderfully when one of the tube trains which passes in a rush of noises and headlights at the foot of the playing fields stopped, illuminating for the surprised passengers Jeff's suddenly motionless bum.

This was capped one night by Matt Johnson's disgusted reminiscence of a stag night organised for local worthies he had attended in an East End pub once, where the stripper, after her act, entertained members of the audience on stage, though most were too drunk to perform. The point of these stories is not that most or even some policemen are distinguished by their sexual voracity (though it is at least possible that, like young nurses, they tend to exorcise some of the horrors of their job that way), but that there exists a pretty gross, though respectable, sub-culture outside the job. Policemen behaving like animals don't feel like policmen, but like members of the public.

Jeff was only about five foot six though ferociously muscled. He gave me the best account of police violence in arrests that I ever heard: 'A couple of weeks back we got a call to a burglary. I chased one of these blokes about a quarter of a mile through the hedges and back gardens and then I caught him. He picked up a shovel and started to make a fight of it. So I disarmed him; broke his nose; did a few other things too. What I reckon is that if someone comes quietly, then that's all right. But if they try to hurt me, I don't bother with rules.'

In other words, he was prepared to use as much force as he, rather than a jury, felt was necessary to subdue the man and persuade him that threatening policemen with shovels was imprudent as well as naughty. Perhaps, being short, he felt this more strongly than most of his colleagues. But all would agree that the proper judge of the force justified when threatened is the man who is about to be clouted with a shovel, not the man who hears the story. And the woman in whose back garden the fight took place came out to congratulate him afterwards: 'Most people, the overwhelming majority of people, I think, are on our side.'

Despite its reputation, I doubt if the Met is a particularly violent Force. If it is, the other police forces of Britain must recruit from Gandhians. But in any society in which people hit one another, the police will be among those getting hit; and they will throw some punches themselves. What's interesting is the way in which the police in Britain, and especially the Met, have acquired a reputation for increasing brutality. It's at least possible that police violence becomes excessive in periods of social transition: violence, like other forms of social behaviour, is usually controlled by unspoken codes. These, like most other social codes, have dissolved over the last twenty years, and are still reforming in different ways and at different rates. One reason that the reading classes are so horrified by stories of police brutality is that they don't hit their own children. Nowadays they seldom even send their children away to be beaten at expensive schools. Lacking the experience of codified violence, they tend to suppose that it is all uncontrolled and potentially anarchic.

The old working-class code held that it was perfectly all right to beat your children, and a fair proportion of the older style of policeman would have thought the same. This would have given them a rough code for dealing with adult delinquents, which those beaten up would themselves understand. Matt Johnson remembered how, when he was once charging-sergeant, a prisoner had said to him: 'I shot the cunt. But he was out of order. He grassed me up.' This was one Christmas; and Johnson later went to the pub across the road to get a bottle for his prisoners.

I don't want to sentimentalise gangsters who use shotguns. If there is any one attitude or insight which cuts the police off from the general public, it is their knowledge that what is illegal is usually also immoral. Crime hurts innocent people – which is one of those gigantic, important platitudes which are almost incommunicable except by experience. Yet both Matt and the man with the shotgun would have known what was meant by 'out of order'. That shared understanding turned at times into the sort of shared corruption that Robert Mark took so much trouble to extirpate. Yet something like it is a necessary condition of a civilised society, in which the police are felt, and feel themselves, to be an integral as well as a necessary part.

Policing is by its nature a moral profession: 'Thou shalt not kill' is a law as well as a moral injunction; and to enforce the one entails enforcing the other. But it is also very closely tied to the general morality of society. The police cannot impose new standards: they can merely improve existing ones, which they share, a little at a time.

That was the reasoning behind Sir Robert Peel's principle that the police should be recruited from among the upper working classes, who would themselves have been tempted by, and have rejected, the sort of crimes they would have to deal with. But that sort of culture – which a woman policeman from the East End once exemplified when she said, 'I'm old-fashioned Labour, which isn't socialism. I can't stand socialism. I'm Labour – ' has now disappeared. Nor would it have helped the old-fashioned police very much when dealing with mobs; and any crowd can feel like a mob if you do not sympathise with its purposes.

So an old-fashioned policeman faced with, say, a demonstration against the Vietnam war would have been in the first place frightened no matter how law-abiding the demonstrators intended to be : imagine losing touch with a small child in a rush-hour crowd in a tube station to see how frightening even the most innocent crowd can seem, and how threatening in its complete imperviousness to individual human purpose.

In the second place, such a policeman, faced with a political demonstration, would have been confronted with something outside his own experience. Given something both frightening and strange, the impulse to reduce it to something he could understand, and if necessary hit to bring under control, must have been strong.

Most law-abiding people base their opinion of the police on their first five minutes' experience. If that is bad, then the whole Force is damned. While I was writing this book, the barrister son of a respectable friend of mine was pointlessly arrested in the West End for irritating a policeman who had irritated him. His father at once started writing articles to demand that the police be brought under democratic control. To him, it confirmed all his darkest imaginings about the Met as overbearing yobs in uniform. And perhaps the men who arrested his son were louts. A dull patrol at three in the morning, in a cramped car, brings out the lout in everyone. But when I heard the story I felt certain that it could all have been avoided. A little attempt to find the human being behind the uniform would have done the trick, and if not behind the first uniform, then the second or third. Of course, I had the advantage of knowing that there are human beings there, so much so that I scarcely saw the uniforms.

Jeff came in one day bitter after being rebuked for an excess of zeal; 'I'm not anti-homosexual. My mate Mike is gay, and I go round there for tea sometimes. He lives with his boyfriend. But Mike says he'd never go to a toilet to pick someone up. Anyway, there we were, with fifteen complaints in one week about a toilet. They were touching up the kids as well. So Matt set up an observation with me. And after a while we saw these two blokes. They were buggering each other. Yeah, they were doing it when we came in.

'And when we got back here the roof fell in on us. Didn't we know we weren't to do observations without permission? And not on toilets without orders from the DAC? And always one of us in uniform?

'We can hardly do anything now without checking to make sure we're not interfering with something political.'

This attitude to gays seemed fairly widespread. A number of people had sympathetic memories of pathetic married men who had been caught cottaging. They did not feel these people deserved a public humiliation. But they resented here, as elsewhere, being unable to make their own decisions about what needed doing. And sexual abuse of teenagers seemed to them unforgivable. I nearly wrote 'sexual abuse of innocents', but when the matter came up, it was more complicated than that.

It started with a dirty photograph. 'It's over-exposed, or the lens is steamed up, but you can see it's her minge all right,' said Matt Johnson. It was of a girl of about thirteen wearing nothing below the waist, and it had been found in the pocket of an old man with a very long criminal record who was regarded as a 'very good printer', which means a forger rather than a member of the NGA.

He also had 'three bent MOTs' on him when stopped in his van. The question that fascinated the PPG was whether he could be done for more. They had no doubt he should be. Once they had followed him to a rendezvous with strangers who turned out to be Robbery squad detectives, who used him as an informant.

Possession of the photograph was in itself illegal. But it seemed unlikely that anyone would take photographs and do no more. A number of girls used to come to his flat on the worst estate on the ground. Only one would co-operate: the girl in the photograph.

She regarded him as a sort of uncle, a dispenser of treats. His protection might be dispensed with if the police could offer more. She was thirteen, but sometimes she looked about sixteen, sometimes nearly ten. Her mouth was painted. Her dark hair fell in tresses like a Kate Greenaway figure. She had dark eyes, occasionally ruffled by thought. She would say whatever she thought was expected; and this at first meant stout protestations of innocence. But she was not very good at working out what was expected. It became clear that the problem in interrogating her was not so much to get her to co-operate, but to introduce her to the idea that there might be a difference between true and false statements, and that she was being asked for true ones.

Her mother and stepfather came with her to the station: a heavy-set couple with bad teeth and numerous children by several marriages, bewildered and in pain, yet trying to do their best. They sat in the canteen while vehement Jeff was absolutely sweet to them. There is no other adjective for his consideration. So much for first impressions. They waited there because they thought their child might find it easier to tell a stranger what had been done to her. She was questioned in the senior officers' dining room: we sat round the long polished wooden table, and when she tossed her head and smiled it seemed as if she were trying to turn the proceedings into a dolls' tea party. She held her glass of water with both hands.

The stories came out hugger-mugger, and tangled where they crossed one another. Yes she had done this. No she never done that, honest. It was her friend done that. Well he kept this cream in the van, and rubbed her

155

with it. And then, one afternoon he had. Yes she knew what she meant. She'd done it with another boy once. No, her parents didn't know about it.

Matt Johnson went out to break the news to her parents. There was none of the usual sense of achievement at the end of an interrogation. She'd just told a circumstantial dirty story which would not stand up in court. There was an awful clarity about what she was trying to say: she knew the sort of thing he'd done; but a great vagueness about the anatomical detail.

While her mother stopped weeping, and arranged to take the other children home, and her stepfather talked with her quietly, Matt asked me what I thought. I said the story proved nothing except that the old man liked the company of retarded teenage girls. 'That', he said 'means every girl on the estate.'

At last the practical things were settled, and we drove the girl to a police surgeon some miles away, in a quiet, leafy street, to see if she was telling the truth. The examination took about half an hour, while her stepfather and I made conversation outside the car. It was the sort of summer evening that makes you feel good to be alive. He could hardly afford to work, being in the poverty trap. He loved his wife, and he was trying to look after his family, and he did not complain. There was nothing I could do about the awful intimacy thrust on us. He seemed stoical, until the child came out. Quick, quiet conversation established that what she had described was anatomically impossible. On the way back, she sat with her father in the back seat, once more about ten years old, prattling away: 'Ooh it hurt ever so much when she touched me there! Look, Dad, look, a horse!'

I remembered Jeff's saying: if you can't take a joke, you shouldn't have been born.

Afterword

Six months later I left a lecture given by the Bishop of Oxford, headed for the nearest pub, and found it full of Chelsea CID. They were having a noisy leaving party for one of their number. I recognised them by their hands and by the way in which they returned my interested gaze. They looked interested back, rather than shifty or aggressive. The whole time I was writing this book, people I met would ask me 'What are the police like?' And about the only answer I could find to that question that would hold good for all policemen was that you can spot them by watching their hands and their eyes. I could have said that I liked them: that I found them honest and interesting, once they thought I was on their side; but on the occasions when I tried that line of argument some people thought I was trying to be clever. People who have never had occasion to be frightened of criminals do not seem to think it possible to like the police. I, who could no longer see policemen as other than individuals, who must be individually approached, expect now to enjoy and to learn from the company of about one in three. This is certainly a higher average than journalists or clergymen would score.

I introduced myself to the CID. One told me that as a merchant seaman he had once played football with Bob Marley in Jamaica, and afterwards shared a spliff with him. But first – of course – I had to satisfy their curiosity. What they wanted to know was what I was trying to prove: what was my angle? And here again I was at a loss. I had wanted to write about the job; to make plain how the police can shape their work, and how their work shapes them. I had thought that I could watch, and then show, their reactions to a whole series of crimes.

Yet looking back, I felt that, largely, I had failed, and I could not decide whether this failure was a consequence of the nature of police work. Certainly I had got the time scale wrong. The idea that anyone could be caught, tried and sentenced within four months for anything more serious than a parking offence seemed ludicrous now. It was sometimes – perhaps often – possible to follow the progress of an investigation, because only the most important crimes are looked at for very long. But the jump between knowledge and judicial conviction is vast. There is hardly a successful arrest in the book. It's almost all about the necessary frustrations of the job, and how hugely satisfying they are. I suppose that must have been my angle all along.

Bayswater, May 1987